THE FALL OF COMMUNISM

Germany: United Again

by Jeffrey B. Symynkywicz

Dillon Press • Parsippany, New Jersey

To my parents, with deep gratitude

Credits
Cover: The Bettmann Archive

AP/Wide World Photos: 25, 39, 50, 53, 58, 82, 84, 87. The Bettmann
Archive: 8, 13, 14, 22, 29, 34, 35, 43, 46, 65, 73, 77, 90, 102, 112.
Culver Pictures: 12, 19. Liaison International: 108; Patrick Piel: 60, 95.
Photo Reporters/DPA: 69. Map by Ortelius Design: 4.

Library of Congress Cataloging-in-Publication Data
Symynkywicz, Jeffrey.
  Germany, united again / by Jeffrey B. Symynkywicz. —   1st ed.
    p. cm. — (The fall of communism)
    Includes bibliographical references and index.
    ISBN 0-87518-634-3. — ISBN 0-382-39190-X (pbk.)
    1. Germany—History—Unification, 1990—Juvenile literature.
  2. German reunification question (1949–1990)—Juvenile literature.
  3. Germany—Politics and government—1990—Juvenile literature.
  4. Germany (East)—Politics and government—1989–1990—Juvenile
literature. [1. Germany—History—Unification, 1990. 2. Germany—
Politics and government—1990-] I. Title. II. Series.
DD290.29.S96 1996
943.087'9—dc20   95-14449

Summary: An account of the reunification of Germany, providing an
overview of modern German history and highlighting both the events that
culminated in the unification of the divided nation and the challenges faced
by the German people today.

Published by Dillon Press,
A Division of Simon & Schuster
299 Jefferson Road, Parsippany, NJ 07054

First edition

Printed in the United States of America

10 9 8 7 6 5 4 3 2 1

CONTENTS

GERMANY (before reunification)

⊛ National capital ○ Other city
East Germany West Germany
BERLIN INSET
American British
French Russian

BERLIN INSET
French Sector
British Sector
WEST BERLIN
American Sector
EAST BERLIN
Russian Sector
EAST GERMANY
EAST GERMANY

DENMARK

N
W E
S

NORTH SEA

BALTIC SEA

Hamburg
Elbe River

GERMAN DEMOCRATIC REPUBLIC

POLAND

NETHER-LANDS

FEDERAL REPUBLIC OF GERMANY

BERLIN ⊛

Rhine River

Leipzig ○

Dresden ○

BONN

Frankfurt ○

BELGIUM

CZECHOSLOVAKIA

LUXEMBOURG

Danube River

FRANCE

Munich ○

AUSTRIA

SWITZERLAND

0   100

chapter 1

Berlin, October 3, 1990

Few could believe it had happened so quickly. The German people called the peaceful revolution that had swept the country *die Wende*, the turning point. And, indeed, during the previous 11 months, the people of Germany had witnessed changes of mammoth proportions.

From 1945 to 1990, Germany had been a divided country. Two German states, East and West, with completely different social and political systems, had existed side by side, separated by an often hostile boundary. The city of Berlin, before 1945 the capital of the entire German nation, lay 110 miles inside the eastern German state. It too was divided between East and West. A massive wall of grey concrete, topped with barbed wire, ran right through its center—a clear, unmistakable sign of Germany's division.

For 45 years this division had stood. Although politicians in both Germanys made references in their speeches to "one German people" and the "united German fatherland," most Germans had largely given up hope that they would once again see a united Germany. Even as late as 1988, West Germany's chancellor, Helmut Kohl, had voiced this negative view as he responded to a reporter's question about whether he would experience unification in his own lifetime: "No, probably I will not live to see it."[1]

But within a year of Kohl's comment, the reunification of Germany had become a real possibility. Only two years later, on the night of October 2, 1990, just hours before the reunification of Germany was to become official, Chancellor Kohl spoke to the German people. East Germans and West Germans who watched him on television saw the chancellor's eyes fill with tears as he addressed them.

"In a few hours," he said, "a dream will become reality. After 40 bitter years of division, Germany, our fatherland, will be reunited. This is one of the happiest moments of my life. . . . I know this great joy is felt by the vast majority of you as well."[2]

At the same time that Kohl was speaking, the national legislature of East Germany was gathering one last time. The final order of business for the assembly was officially to dissolve the German Democratic Republic (GDR), as the eastern part of Germany had been called since 1949.

A few of the deputies spoke of how disappointed they were that the GDR was to be absorbed into the larger Federal Republic of Germany (FRG). They mourned the loss of their nation—the only nation some of them had ever known. Most of those present, however, eagerly anticipated unification with the West and shared the sentiments expressed on the occasion by East Germany's prime minister, Lothar de Maizière. De Maizière, the only non-Communist, freely elected prime minister in the GDR's history, uttered the final words—delivered the eulogy, so to speak—for the East German state. His words echoed those spoken by Chancellor Kohl just a short time before:

"In a few moments," remarked de Maizière, "the German Democratic Republic accedes to the Federal Republic of Germany. With that, we Germans achieve unity in freedom. It is an hour of great joy. It is the end of many illusions. It is a farewell without tears."[3]

Then the Berlin Symphony Orchestra performed the Ninth Symphony of Ludwig von Beethoven, one of the most famous German composers of all time. Soon the music of the symphony's final movement, the stirring "Ode to Joy," filled the Schauspielhaus, Berlin's huge concert hall. All those present sang along.

The words, by the German poet Friedrich von Schiller, were familiar to nearly all Germans, Easterners and Westerners alike—Ossis and Wessis, as they called each other:

> *Joy, thou goddess, fair, immortal,*
> *Offspring of Elysium,*
> *Mad with rapture, to the portal*
> *of thy holy fane we come!*

In recent days, some observers noted, a few Germans had even taken to substituting Freiheit (freedom) for Freude (joy) as they sang the words of the well-known anthem.

Outside the hall where dignitaries sang of joy and freedom, in the streets of Berlin, the general feeling was joy and jubilation. On both sides of Berlin's much-hated Wall, hundreds of thousands had gathered to celebrate the reunification of their nation. Perhaps a million were gathered in the large plaza in front of the Reichstag building, which had housed Germany's parliament before the country was divided. To some, it seemed to take forever for the appointed hour of unity to arrive.

Finally, as clocks struck midnight, a replica of the American Liberty Bell, a gift to the city of West Berlin from the government of the United States, rang out in the cool October night. At that same moment, the black, red, and gold flag of the Federal Republic of Germany was hoisted up the tall flagpole at the front of the Reichstag. A million German voices sang out together the words of their national anthem:

> *Unity and justice and freedom*
> *For the German fatherland...*

Fireworks then set the sky over Berlin ablaze as the celebrations continued. Bottles of champagne were uncorked; mugs of rich German beer were lifted high. All along Berlin's main boulevard, Unter den Linden, the shouts and singing of thousands of happy citizens blended with the different music of numerous bands, creating a loud and happy confusion.

Fireworks explode over the Brandenburg Gate in Berlin as East and West Germany celebrate their reunification on October 3, 1990.

Not all of those gathered in the streets of Berlin that night were celebrating, however. Shortly after the reunification of Germany was proclaimed, several thousand protesters gathered in West Berlin's Kreuzberg district, just over the Wall from the East. Many were there to protest what they believed was a "sell-out" by East Germany's leaders to the capitalist West. Others wanted to remind their nation's leaders and people of the evil that had come about in the past when German nationalism went unchecked. The banners they carried and the slogans they shouted gave voice to their fears. One banner read "Germany Shut Up! That's Enough." Another made reference to Germany's tragic past. It read "Never again Germany." Never again, the protester declared, should Germany be allowed to conquer and control other peoples in pursuit of its own national interests.

The protesters made their way out of the Kreuzberg area and across the Landwehr Canal, and east toward where the Wall still stood. Then the marchers, now numbering several thousand, made their way into the city's eastern sector. There the loud, unruly throng continued to shout their slogans of defiance. But by now the crowd celebrating the rebirth of a united Germany had grown so large and exuberant and loud that the protesters were almost completely ignored.

While the large body of police guarding the protest demonstrations managed to keep most of the marchers under control, one large group calling itself Autonome managed to avoid the watchful eyes of the authorities. Autonome had become well known around Berlin over the past several months. To some, it seemed as though this radical group had attempted to disturb every recent ceremony celebrating the approaching reunification of the country. Now, only a few hours into the existence of a newly reunited Germany, these same protesters were showing their unhappiness by rampaging through East Berlin's large central square, the Alexanderplatz, smashing the windows of shops and offices and even overturning parked automobiles.

The Berlin police moved quickly to restore calm. Five thousand additional officers were summoned to the area around the Alexanderplatz. At first, the young radicals resisted police attempts to restore order, but soon they proved no match for the authorities and dispersed before the police's water cannons and tear gas.

By early the next morning, Berlin was quiet again. The only people who remained in the center of the city were the street cleaners. What a massive job they faced: sweeping clean streets that had been crowded with thousands just hours before, collecting huge amounts of trash from the city's parks, and clearing tons of broken bottles and empty beer cans from the area around the Reichstag building and the Brandenburg Gate.

As the street cleaners labored busily, a new day dawned. Germany was a united land again after more than four decades of division. A national holiday was declared to celebrate the first full day of German unity. Hundreds of thousands of Germans in cities across the land took to the streets again, to celebrate and sing and to talk with one another about the road that lay ahead.

Some believed that unity had come about too quickly, without adequate opportunity to consider all of its possible effects. Others feared that the future costs of reunification and the rebuilding of the former East Germany might eventually bankrupt the country. Still others—both in Germany and beyond its borders—quietly shared the fear of the young protesters who had demonstrated so loudly the night before: that a powerful, unified German state might once again develop into a dangerous, unstable force in the heart of Europe.

No one, of course, could state with certainty what the reunification of Germany would mean in years ahead. Some observers looked at the events of October 3, 1990, and saw the defeat of tyranny and a great victory for freedom. Others who looked at the same events feared the rise of uncontrolled nationalism and the eventual triumph of extremist views. But whatever happened, now that Germany was united again, Europe—and the world—would never be the same.

chapter 2

Dreams of Empire

T he German nation had a long history of division and discord. Between the years 1300 and 1500, strong national monarchies had assumed power throughout Europe, most notably in England and France. Germany, however, resisted this movement toward unity. It would take several centuries longer to forge the German lands—described by one historian as "a crazy quilt of kingdoms, duchies, bishoprics, free cities, and other flotsam"[1]—into a single united empire. Finally, on January 18, 1871, in a grand ceremony at the Palace of Versailles, just outside of Paris, King Wilhelm of Prussia was proclaimed the first kaiser, or emperor, of a new German Empire. The coming of World War I in 1914, however, would spell this empire's downfall.

For four years, bitter fighting raged across Europe. Two rival alliances, the Triple Alliance (Germany, Italy, and Austria-Hungary) and the Triple Entente (Britain, France, and Russia), were pitted against each other. During fighting on the western front in France, Germany suffered heavy losses. Then in 1917, the United States joined the war against Germany. Finally, by late 1918, the German people had had enough. On October 28, when the German fleet was ordered to sail from its headquarters at Wilhelmshaven, thousands of sailors refused to fight any longer. Soon the Wilhelmshaven mutiny had spread to the entire German fleet, and within days the whole country was in the

German reservists leaving for war in early September 1914.

throes of rebellion against the kaiser. The government resigned and fled to safety in the Netherlands.

On November 9, 1918, a new German Republic was proclaimed in Berlin. The new socialist government under Friedrich Ebert immediately sued for peace. Two days later, representatives of the German military command traveled to the headquarters of French Marshall Ferdinand Foch, general-in-chief of the Entente armies, in the Compiègne Forest, in northeastern France. There, in an old railway car, they signed an armistice. A few hours later, at 11:00 A.M. on Monday, November 11, 1918, the fighting stopped. World War I was over at last.

German soldiers in trenches man machine guns on the
fortified banks of the Vistula River.

The armistice that ended World War I was signed in an old railway car in the Compiègne Forest in France.

The terms accepted by Germany at Compiègne were quite harsh. German troops were to surrender their weapons and warships immediately and retreat from all occupied territory in Belgium, Luxembourg, and France. Furthermore, Entente troops were to be allowed to occupy Germany to enforce the terms of peace. Through the armistice, the Entente gained entry into German territory—something they had not been able to achieve through years of fighting.

The new republican government in Germany faced enormous challenges. Thousands of troops needed to be demilitarized. Continuing rebellions all across the country needed to be put down. The economy needed to be rebuilt, and adequate supplies of food, fuel, and other necessities of life had to be guaranteed. And an entirely new government structure had to be put into place. In the face of these overwhelming challenges, the new German Constituent Assembly gathered in the city of Weimar in February 1919. Friedrich Ebert was confirmed as president, and Philipp Scheidemann was named prime minister.

Representatives of the government then traveled to Paris to finalize a peace agreement. The treaty signed at Versailles on June 28 imposed a high price for Germany's military defeat. Vast areas of territory—including Alsace-Lorraine, West Prussia, and Upper Silesia—were lost. Lost, too, were Germany's colonies in Africa and the Pacific. The size of the German army was severely limited, and German troops could not be stationed in the Rhineland bordering on France. In addition, Germany and Austria were forbidden from ever uniting into a single nation. Worst of all, perhaps, Germany had to admit "war guilt"—blame for causing World War I— and so agreed to pay the victorious Entente billions of dollars in reparations.

Many Germans were very angry when they heard the terms of peace accepted by their government. Some believed that Germany should refuse to accept such harsh dictates and should take up arms again to defend German honor. Most Germans, however, understood how weak and divided the war had left their land. Many believed that their country could be rebuilt and its prosperity restored only in peace.

▼ ▲ ▼

The leaders of the Weimar Republic worked hard to rebuild Germany and to meet the terms of the Treaty of Versailles. However, they faced staunch opposition from within their own country. German Communists accused the government's leaders of favoring the interests of the nation's wealthy industrialists and bankers at the expense of working people and the poor. Other more conservative forces longed for the restoration of the kaiser and the empire and blamed the socialist government at Weimar for Germany's defeat in World War I. According to this view, the German army had not been beaten in battle; rather, Germany had lost the war only because it had been "stabbed in the back" by traitors at home who had risen in revolution, overthrown the kaiser, and then accepted shameful terms of peace.

The new government also faced major financial troubles. At the conclusion of the war, the German unit of currency, the mark, had been valued at four to the U.S. dollar. However, its value quickly began to plummet: By the summer of 1921, the mark had dropped to 75 to the dollar; by the next year, 400. But the government continued to print money to meet its expenses and its obligation to pay reparations. Inflation drove the value of the mark lower as prices of goods rose accordingly. In January 1923, it took 18,000 German marks to make a dollar; by July 1 of the same year, 160,000; by August 1, 1 million; and by November, 4 billion. The German currency had become completely worthless.

Late in 1923 the government of Prime Minister Gustav Stresemann introduced a new currency, the Rentenmark, and implemented financial policies that finally brought the runaway inflation under control. However, with the coming of the Great

Depression in 1929, the German economy again took a turn for the worse. Between September 1929 and September 1930, unemployment doubled and then continued to rise. By 1933, over 6 million Germans—one third of the entire work force—were without jobs.

To many, the Weimar government seemed completely unable to cope with such awesome challenges. Different political parties fought continually among themselves. They seemed unable to reach agreement on anything at all. More and more Germans began to lose faith in their government and looked toward more radical political groups to rescue their country from its woes.

In September 1930, one of these groups, the National Socialist German Workers Party—known as the Nazis—gained 107 seats in elections for the German parliament, the Reichstag. However, the socialist Social Democratic Party was still the parliament's largest group, and the Communists too gained additional seats. Many of Germany's wealthy businessmen and industrialists feared that the radical forces of the left might be on the verge of gaining power. They began to look toward the Nazis as allies in the fight against a socialist takeover.

In the German presidential election of 1932, the Nazi leader, Adolf Hitler, decided to challenge the sitting president, Paul von Hindenburg. Hitler was defeated but was able to gain more than 36 percent of the vote—a significant showing. The Nazis' strength continued to grow. In elections for the Reichstag in July 1932, the Nazis emerged as the assembly's largest party, with a total of 230 seats. Hitler was now ready to try to take over the government.

Some conservative leaders in Germany, including former chancellor Franz von Papen, believed that bringing Hitler into the government would be the best way to control him. They mistakenly believed that, once in power as part of a conservative coalition, Hitler would face the responsibility of governing and would tone down the Nazis' more radical activities. In August, Papen persuaded Hindenburg to offer Hitler the government post of vice-chancellor. Hitler refused the offer: He was not willing to settle for second place. In January 1933, Hitler held a series of meetings with Papen and Hindenburg. As a result of these talks, Hindenburg agreed to allow Hitler to form a government. On January 30, 1933, Adolf Hitler became chancellor of Germany.

▼ ▲ ▼

Hitler lost no time in establishing a dictatorship. On February 27, 1933, the Reichstag building went up in flames. Immediately the Nazis accused the Communists of setting the fire. (Almost all historians now believe that the Nazis themselves were responsible for the fire.) Using the fire—and the threat of a Communist takeover that it supposedly represented—as an excuse, Hitler persuaded Hindenburg to sign the "Law for Removing the Distress of the People and Reich." This law, which became known as the Enabling Act, would be disastrous for democracy in Germany. Even though the Reichstag continued to meet, the right to draft laws, approve the national budget, and establish foreign policy now passed into the hands of the chancellor and his cabinet. Furthermore, the Enabling Act even stated that the chancellor's decrees "might deviate from the constitution" if they needed to!

Within a year, all political parties except the Nazi Party were outlawed. The press, labor unions, and much of the economy were placed under Nazi control. No criticism of the government was tolerated, and Hitler's secret police, the Gestapo, ruthlessly punished all real or imagined enemies. Jews were singled out for special persecution. Within months of assuming office, Hitler issued decrees banning Jews from holding government, professional, or university positions. He proclaimed a national boycott of Jewish shops and businesses. By 1935, all Jews in Germany had their citizenship revoked and became subjects of the state. An even more ominous development, however, was the establish-

Adolf Hitler reviewing troops

ment of a special system of prison camps for Hitler's political enemies, as well as for social "undesirables" such as gypsies, homosexuals, and the physically and mentally handicapped.

When General von Hindenburg died in August 1934, Hitler combined the offices of president and chancellor and named himself *Führer* (leader) of the German nation. He called his "New Order" the Third Reich, or Third German Empire. It was to be even more glorious than its predecessors, the Holy Roman Empire and the German Empire of Bismarck. Furthermore,

Hitler predicted the Third Reich would last for a thousand years and would transform the face of Germany. In reality, it would last 12 years, 4 months, and 8 days. When it ended, Germany would lie in total ruin.

With complete political control secured, Hitler turned to his dreams of conquest. The German people needed *Lebensraum*, Hitler declared, "living space"—room to develop and grow. This "living space" was to be taken from the Jews, Slavs, and other non-Nordic, "inferior" peoples of Europe.

In the early years of his campaigns, Hitler achieved notable political and diplomatic victories while the rest of Europe sat back and did little. In complete disregard of the Treaty of Versailles, he rebuilt the German armed forces into the strongest in Europe and sent troops to reoccupy the Rhineland, on the border with France. In March 1938, Germany annexed Austria. Six months later, the Germans seized the Sudetenland from Czechoslovakia. A year later the rest of Czechoslovakia came under German control.

When Hitler invaded Poland in September 1939, Great Britain and France felt they had no choice but to go to war with Germany. Poland fell quickly to the Germans. By May 1940, Belgium, Denmark, Luxembourg, Holland, and Norway had all fallen to Nazi Germany's *Blitzkreig*, a war that moved at lightning speed and with all of lightning's destructive force. Hitler then attacked France with similar success. In little more than a month, the French government of Marshall Henri Pétain sued for peace. Hitler marched triumphantly through the streets of Paris as the German swastika flew over the Eiffel Tower. Most of France's territory was placed under the direct control of the German army. Pétain was given control of a smaller area in the south, with its capital at Vichy.

Eventually, however, the tide of the war turned against Germany. In June 1941, Hitler launched an invasion of the Soviet Union, and German troops advanced hundreds of miles into Soviet territory. They were finally stopped, by the

Soviet Red Army and the bitter Russian winter, just a few miles outside of Moscow. In December of the same year, following the bombing of Pearl Harbor by Germany's ally Japan, the United States entered the war. In May 1943, after a hard fight, the Allies drove the Germans out of North Africa. The Allies then gained control of Sicily, from which they launched an invasion of mainland Italy. Troops landed in Calabria, in Italy's far south, on September 3, 1943. The Italian dictator Benito Mussolini, Hitler's close ally, fell from power, and Italy's new government quickly sought peace with the Allies. Hitler then dispatched nearly half a million troops to the south to retake Italy. For almost a year the two invading armies struggled against each other. Finally, on June 4, 1944, Rome fell to the Allies.

Two days later was D Day. On June 6, 1944, a combined British, Canadian, and American force of nearly 3 million troops landed at Normandy, along France's western coast. Now, Germany faced enemies to the east, west, and south, as well as massive bombardment from the air. The end of the Third Reich was only a matter of time.

By September 12, 1944, the U.S. First Army had crossed into German territory. However, it was not until March of 1945 that it was able to cross the Rhine and head toward Berlin, with other Allied armies right behind it.

Meanwhile, in the east, the Soviet Red Army had turned back the last German offensive on Moscow in July 1943 and had steadily regained all of the lost lands. One after another, the Crimea, the Ukraine, Byelorussia, eastern Poland, and Lithuania passed from the hands of Germany. In October 1944, Finland surrendered and joined the war on the Allied side. By March 1945, three other states aligned with Germany—Romania, Bulgaria, and Hungary—had also withdrawn from the war in the face of advancing Soviet troops.

In February 1945 the Soviet dictator Josef Stalin hosted a meeting with the American president Franklin Roosevelt and the British prime minister Winston Churchill at the resort city of Yalta

At the Yalta Conference in February 1945, the Allied leaders made plans for Europe after the war. In the front row of this picture, from left to right, are British Prime Minister Winston Churchill, U.S. President Franklin D. Roosevelt, and Soviet Premier Josef Stalin.

in the Soviet Crimea. At the Yalta Conference, plans were made for Europe after the war. While most of the discussions centered on questions related to Poland, other matters were considered, including who should control Germany once Hitler was toppled. At an earlier conference at Tehran in Iran in 1943, the Allies had agreed that once a military victory was achieved in Europe, Germany should be divided into three separate "occupation zones," controlled by Britain, the United States, and the Soviet Union. At Yalta the three Allied leaders once again endorsed the idea of establishing occupation zones. In addition, Churchill and Roosevelt insisted that a French zone be established.

Over the next few months, events moved quickly as Hitler finally conceded that the end of the Reich was near. On March 19, 1945, the Führer declared a policy of "scorched earth." He told Albert Speer, one of his chief advisors: "If the war is lost, the nation will also perish." Hitler then issued a decree calling for the destruction of "all industrial plants, all important electrical facilities, waterworks, gasworks, food stores, and clothing stores; all bridges, all railway and communication installations, all waterways, all ships, all freight cars, and all locomotives."[2]

But Hitler was no longer in a position to enforce such a horrible order. Enemy troops, in the east and west alike, were now within a few miles of Berlin, and Germany's troops were in full retreat across Europe. Only a few fanatical advisors remained with Hitler in his fortified bunker beneath Berlin's chancellery. Here, on April 12, he received news of the death of the American president Roosevelt. Perhaps this was a sign from heaven, the Nazi propaganda chief Joseph Goebbels told Hitler. But within a few days these delusions were shattered. On April 22, Soviet troops broke through the German defensive line and entered the city limits of Berlin. After a week of house-to-house fighting, they were within a block of Hitler's fortress. The Nazi leader saw at last that his end had come, and on April 30, 1945, he committed suicide.

The Third Reich survived just one more week. On May 7, one of the leading German commanders, General Alfred Jodl, came to the headquarters of the Allied commander Dwight Eisenhower. There, he signed Germany's unconditional surrender. The war in Europe was over.

chapter 3

A Land Divided

After the war, Germany faced a massive job of rebuilding. Nearly every major city lay in rubble. In some places, most houses had been destroyed. Industry was at a standstill; agriculture was in a shambles. There were severe shortages of food, medicine, and most other basics. In many places the water supply had been contaminated. And all institutions of the German state, including schools, police, and the courts, had fallen along with Hitler. Only the presence of several armies of occupation maintained a semblance of order.

In July 1945, just two months after Germany's surrender, the Allied leaders gathered in Potsdam, 16 miles outside of Berlin, for another summit conference. A new president, Harry S. Truman, represented the United States. Nine days after the conference began, British prime minister Winston Churchill was beaten in parliamentary elections at home. He was replaced at Potsdam by Clement Attlee, leader of the opposition Labor Party. Of the powerful trio that had deliberated at Yalta only the ruthless Stalin remained.

At Potsdam, differences between the victors came into the open. The British and Americans accused the Soviets of breaking the promise they had made at Yalta to allow free elections in lands under their control. For his part, Stalin demanded the major share of the $20 billion in damages the Germans owed. The Soviets did agree, however, to implement the plan to set up

German women clean up war rubble in 1945 on Tauentzine Street in Berlin where the U.S. and British sectors meet.

four occupation zones in Germany. They also agreed that the German capital, Berlin—110 miles inside the Soviet zone— would be divided into separate Allied zones as well. All the participants at Potsdam agreed that the division of Germany was to be temporary and that Germany should never again be able to threaten the peace of Europe. But they differed widely on the best way to achieve this goal.

The Allies also dealt with the economies in their sectors differently. The Soviets had suffered terrible devastation at the hands of the invading Germans. Receiving damages, or reparations, from their defeated foe became their first priority. Under the terms of the Potsdam agreement, the Soviets were allowed to dismantle German industries and ship their machinery and equipment to the USSR. The agreement also required the other

Allies to provide the Soviets with machinery from industries in their zones. However, the agreement expressly forbade any of the Allies from shipping goods manufactured in Germany back to their lands as credits toward reparations. When the Soviets began doing precisely that, the British and American representatives protested loudly—and were completely ignored by the Soviets.

In retaliation, the American and British commands announced that they would no longer dismantle industries in their zones to benefit the Soviets. Rather, the Western Allies launched policies intended to rebuild Germany's industry and strengthen the country's economy. The Americans and British began to make massive shipments of goods into their zones. They also allowed industries in their areas to produce greater quantities of goods than those allowed under the Potsdam agreement. They stepped up cooperation and increased trade between their two zones as well. This time, it was the Soviets' turn to protest.

Disagreements over Germany were only part of a larger conflict that was now emerging among the former allies. On March 5, 1946, Winston Churchill, speaking at a college graduation in Fulton, Missouri, looked out anxiously at the spread of Communism in Eastern Europe and declared: "From Stetin in the Baltic to Trieste in the Adriatic, an iron curtain has descended across the continent."[1] Almost exactly one year later, on March 12, 1947, President Truman declared that all attempts to impose Communist governments in Europe would meet with the staunch resistance of the United States. A new period in history, the Cold War, had begun.

But the Soviets went forward with their plan to establish a Communist government within their occupation zone. In April 1946, the Socialist Unity Party was formed to further the cause of "socialist democracy" in the East. While the party, known by its German abbreviation as the SED, claimed to be a united front of all anti-Fascist forces, it was, in fact, completely dominated by the German Communist Party led by Walter Ulbricht. Ulbricht was a staunch Stalinist who had spent the war years in Moscow. He had flown back to Berlin on board a Soviet plane in April 1945. Now that the war was over, he was keen on applying the fine points of strategy he had learned from Marshal Stalin himself.

Ulbricht realized that the people of Soviet-occupied Germany would never willingly vote to install a Communist government. He also knew that the German Communist Party was not strong enough to seize control of the eastern zone by itself. So he pressured the leaders of the Social Democratic Party in the Soviet-controlled area to merge with the Communists to form one larger, dominant party and to lead the way in founding a "German road to socialism."

▼ ▲ ▼

Soon after the founding of the Socialist Unity Party, Soviet authorities in Berlin announced that to guard against a resurgence of fascism all political parties had to be "coordinated" within the single "united anti-Fascist front" of the SED. By 1949, all political forces in Soviet-occupied Germany had become part of this united front and were, in effect, under the domination of the Soviets and their German underlings.

As relations between East and West worsened, the situation in Berlin became more complicated as well. The Soviets insisted that the German capital be reunited as part of the Soviet zone in which it was located. The other three Allies, however, were just as insistent that their rights in the city be maintained.

In December 1947, angry words were exchanged between the two sides at a meeting of the Allied Control Council, which had been established to coordinate relations among the four zones. In February 1948 the Soviets announced that they were imposing severe travel restrictions on Westerners traveling through their zone to reach Berlin. The next month, the Soviets withdrew from the Allied Control Council and declared the work of that board finished. Soon the Soviets were also refusing to deliver packages mailed to their zone.

In June, France, Great Britain, and the United States announced that a new German currency—the deutsche mark— was to be issued as the legal means of commerce for all of Berlin. Angered, the Soviets responded on June 23 by issuing a new currency of their own in Berlin—the ostmark. The next day, June 24, 1948, the Soviets moved to seize complete control of the capital.

The Soviets declared that the Western Allies' right to occupy Berlin had been terminated. All British, French, and American troops must leave the city at once. The right to travel across Soviet-occupied eastern Germany to reach Berlin was also sus- pended, and all 80 access routes into the city—road, rail, and water—were sealed off by Soviet troops. Six days later the Soviets turned off Berlin's electrical power and stopped all ship- ments of food and other essential supplies into those parts of the city not under their control. A complete blockade of West Berlin had been instituted.

Some estimated that the city could survive only six weeks without help from the West. Many speculated that the United States, Great Britain, and France would have to accept Soviet demands and withdraw their troops from Berlin.

But Western resolve would not be defeated that easily. Help for Berlin was soon in coming—from the sky. The Allies used airplanes—thousands of them—to launch an airlift to save Berlin. The strategy was a definite gamble. The Soviets might try to shoot down the planes as they flew over "their" part of Germany. There might be terrible loss of life. Would the West retaliate? Would this lead to war?

Many doubted that enough aircraft could be mobilized to sup- ply the people of Berlin—almost 2 million of them—with every- thing they needed for as long as it took the Soviets to reopen road and rail links. But the governments of the West saw no other choice. Early on the morning of June 26, the airlift began. Soon Western aircraft were flying directly over Soviet-controlled territory. At first, there were signs that the Soviets would offer resistance. One of their planes pursued a British plane and opened fire on it. The British craft was knocked from the sky, but the Soviet plane crashed as well, and both crews were killed. Soon it became apparent that the Soviets would offer very little resistance to the airlift. They may have reasoned that it would just not be possible for the West to commandeer enough planes to supply Berlin.

But the airlift continued. Within a month 5,000 flights were coming into West Berlin each week—a rate of one landing every 2 minutes, 24 hours a day, each and every day. All manner of items were being shipped in: food, clothing, medicine—8,000 tons

The Berlin airlift (1948–1949) was successful in bringing supplies to the blockaded city of West Berlin. Here, children wait eagerly for a plane.

of supplies daily. As winter approached and the temperatures began to drop, more planes were added so that heavy bags of coal could be flown into the city. In addition, when the planes returned to the West, many were now crowded with scores of refugees who had decided to leave the hardship in the city.

Finally the Soviet Union realized that its attempt to strangle Berlin had failed. On May 11, 1949, electricity to the city was restored, and lights went on in Berlin for the first time in nearly a year. By the next day, the roadblocks had been lifted, and access to the city by highway, railroad, and canal was again possible.

The West had won the first "battle" of the Cold War, and the survival of democracy in Berlin was secured. However, the Western Allies had grown increasingly suspicious of Soviet intentions and saw the need to guard against further Soviet aggression in Europe. On April 4, 1949, twelve Western nations, including the three Western Allies, formed the North Atlantic Treaty Organization (NATO). The members of NATO agreed to cooperate closely with each other in economic, political, and military matters. They further declared that an attack on any single NATO member state would be considered an attack on all of them. The West would stand together against the Soviet threat.

▼ ▲ ▼

Within Germany, however, West and East continued to drift farther apart. In 1947 the American and British occupation zones had been merged into a single "Bizone." A year later, the French zone joined this common structure. Then, early in 1949, a parliamentary council began meeting in Bonn, a quaint university town on the Rhine River, to draw up a draft constitution for a new West German state.

The council completed its work quickly and submitted the constitution, called the Basic Law, to the Allied powers for acceptance. On May 23, 1949, the formation of the Federal

Republic of Germany (FRG) was officially proclaimed. The constitution of the FRG declared that its ultimate aim was the reunification of all of Germany, with its capital at Berlin. However, in the meantime, Bonn would serve as the provisional capital of the government of the new state.

Germans in the Western part of the country then participated in the first open elections in over 17 years. Two major political parties had developed in West Germany: the staunchly capitalist Christian Democrats and the more socialist-oriented Social Democrats.

In the summer 1948 elections, the Christian Democrats won a narrow victory. In September their leader, Konrad Adenauer, became the first chancellor of the Federal Republic of Germany. Adenauer was a former mayor of Cologne, a large city not far from Germany's westernmost border. He had been an important figure in German politics since the 1930s. During the Hitler years, however, he had gone into retirement and had refused to cooperate with the dictatorship. He had served two brief stints in prison during the war, but in spite of this hardship and the fact that he was 73 years old when called upon to become chancellor, Adenauer nevertheless gave the impression of being a healthy and vigorous man.

The Russians responded to the formation of a sovereign West German state by creating an ally of their own in the East. On October 7, 1949, the German Democratic Republic (GDR) was formed, with the Socialist Unity Party firmly in control. Although the elderly Communist Wilhelm Pieck was named the GDR's first president, no one doubted that Walter Ulbricht, general secretary of the SED, was actually the most powerful man in East Germany.

Under Konrad Adenauer's leadership, West Germany began to emerge from the shadow of military defeat. Adenauer's government sought to strengthen the country's ties to the West and to improve relations with all of its neighbors, especially with Germany's traditional rival, France. A month after Adenauer's swearing-in as chancellor, the FRG became a member of the Organization for European Economic Cooperation. In 1951, West Germany joined the Council of Europe. Eventually, it would become one of the original members of the European Economic Community, the Common Market. In 1955 the Occupation Statute, under which the Allied military command had governed Germany, expired, and the Federal Republic became a completely sovereign state. As such, it was allowed to rebuild its armed forces and became eligible for membership in NATO.

During this time the West German economy was growing rapidly. By 1950, industrial production was once again above prewar levels. Closer cooperation with the West brought new markets and new sources of capital. There was plenty of work for everyone and plenty of goods to buy in shops. New apartment buildings were being built, and cities across West Germany were rising out of the rubble.

West Berlin, in particular, was emerging as an exciting center of commerce, culture, and free expression—right in the heart of the Communist-dominated GDR. Even though the eastern and western parts of the city were under separate governments, it was possible for people in one section to pass readily into the other. Authorities in West Berlin encouraged workers in the eastern part of the city to cross daily into the western sector. The city's economy—especially its construction industry—was growing so fast that a labor shortage had developed there. The West German authorities hoped that these *Grenzgänger*, or "border crossers," from the East would help remedy this problem. Thousands of East German workers were happy to be given the chance to earn good wages and to spend their newly acquired wealth in the better-stocked, better-run shops and businesses of West Berlin. Increasing numbers of *Grenzgänger* were also choosing not to return home to East Berlin when their shifts at work were completed. Instead, many were now asking the West German government for citizenship in the Federal Republic.

Throughout the early 1950s, the number of refugees from East Germany rose rapidly.

In spite of growing dissatisfaction among those who remained behind in East Berlin, the Communist government pressed on with its policies. In June 1953, in a desperate attempt to catch up with the West, Ulbricht ordered an increase in the number of hours that laborers in the construction industry had to work each week—with no increase in wages. Furious workers soon declared a strike and took to the streets of Berlin. Tens of thousands crowded into the Alexanderplatz, East Berlin's central square, demanding an end to the Communist regime. Their rebellion soon spread to cities across the GDR.

The East German police were no match for the thousands of protesters who thronged the streets across the country. In some places, the badly outnumbered police laid down their weapons and joined the side of the protesters! Rioters broke into jails and released political prisoners from their cells. Government offices across East Germany were under siege. Decrees of the Communist government went completely ignored. The workers of the country were now threatening a full-scale armed revolt. Quickly the East German government appealed to its Soviet protector for help. The Soviet response was quick in arriving: Tanks soon were rolling into East Germany's chief cities. The rebellion was crushed, at the cost of more than 800 lives and much of the prestige of the Ulbricht regime. It was now clear just how little support East Germany's Communists enjoyed among their own people. For the first time, the Soviet Union had been forced to intervene militarily in one of its satellites.

Meanwhile, the rush of refugees to the West continued. The Soviets stepped up patrols along the border between East and West Germany. In addition, new barbed-wire fortifications were erected. The situation in Berlin, however, was the Communists' greatest embarrassment. During the 1950s, nearly 3 million East Germans had used the city as a gateway to political asylum in the West. The new Soviet leader, Nikita Khrushchev, declared

Soviet tanks and troops arrive in East Berlin to crush a revolt by East German laborers in 1953.

that Berlin was like an irritating bone lodged in the throat of socialist Germany. Something had to be done.

▼ ▲ ▼

In November 1958, Khrushchev announced that the Allies would be given six months to withdraw their troops from Berlin. After that time, he said, the USSR would sign a separate peace treaty with the GDR. This treaty would recognize the GDR as a fully sovereign nation, which would be granted complete control over its capital city, Berlin. Under Khrushchev's plan, the Allied agreement under which Berlin was governed would be null and void. The entire city would revert to German—that is, East German—control. Following Khrushchev's announcement, tensions again ran very high. As in 1948, some began to speak of the possibility of war—this time with nuclear weapons added to the equation. A second blockade of West Berlin became a distinct possibility. Still, the governments of the West declared that they had no intention of abandoning Berlin.

Again the Soviets backed down. The Soviets did not want war, Khrushchev told an audience in the German city of Leipzig. All they were asking for were "meaningful negotiations." Khrushchev then proposed a summit conference at which the former Allies could work out a peaceful solution to the question of Berlin.

In September 1959, Khrushchev and his family came to the United States at the invitation of President Dwight Eisenhower. On arriving in New York, Khrushchev declared that he had come "with an open heart" so that all the people of the earth should be able to live "in peace and friendship."[2] For nearly two weeks, Khrushchev traveled across the United States, presenting himself as a man of peace—a harmless, warmhearted old man who only wanted a safe, secure world for his grandchildren. For their part, many Americans were impressed by the Soviet leader and the direct, down-to-earth way in which he answered reporters' questions. Khrushchev became a regular feature on

Soviet Premier Nikita Khrushchev with President Eisenhower in Washington during his visit to the United States in September 1959

nightly newscasts: dining in Hollywood with American celebrities like Marilyn Monroe, Bob Hope, and Frank Sinatra; driving an American tractor across a cornfield in Iowa; even bouncing President Eisenhower's grandchildren on his knee at the Eisenhowers' home in Gettysburg, Pennsylvania. Many now forgot the ultimatum concerning Berlin that Khrushchev had issued less than a year before. Perhaps, more Americans now believed, East and West could work out their problems peacefully after all. A summit conference to discuss "the main problems affecting the attainment of peace and stability in the world,"[3] including the question of Berlin, was scheduled to start on May 16, 1960, in the French capital, Paris.

Eleven days before the summit was to begin, on May 5, Khrushchev announced that an American airplane, a U-2, had been shot down deep in Soviet territory and that its pilot had been captured. Eisenhower arrived in Paris to face severe questioning about the U-2 incident. At first, the American government denied that any such mission had been authorized. However, when later confronted with photos of the plane and the captured pilot, Eisenhower had to admit that the downed jet was American. He denied, however, that the U-2 was on a spy mission. When the pilot, Francis Gary Powers, confessed that he was on an espionage mission over the USSR, Eisenhower attempted to defend the need for such spying on the Soviets and even hinted that such missions would continue in the future.

Khrushchev was incensed by what he felt was the betrayal of the new partnership he had formed with Eisenhower during his visit to the United States the previous fall. He probably was also under intense pressure from hard-line Communists, both within the Soviet Union and in Communist China, to toughen his approach to the West.

When the Paris summit conference began at the Elysée Palace on the morning of May 16, Khrushchev immediately demanded that Eisenhower apologize for the U-2 mission and promise to punish those responsible. Eisenhower would promise no more than that such missions would be indefinitely suspended. This was not enough for the Soviet leader. Khrushchev suggested that the conference be postponed for six to eight months, and that Eisenhower's visit to the Soviet Union, scheduled for later that same spring, be postponed as well.

Three days later, Khrushchev held a press conference in Paris and declared that the government of the USSR would not tolerate spy planes flying over its territory. Not only would the Soviet military shoot the planes down, Khrushchev declared, they would also bomb the bases from which the planes had been sent! The next day, Khrushchev flew to East Berlin. There he declared that the Western "occupation" of Berlin could not be tolerated. Meanwhile, the armed forces of the West, fearing a surprise attack by the Soviets, had been placed on full alert.

The Soviet attack never materialized. Instead, Khrushchev again assumed the role of peacemaker. In early June 1961, he met with the new American leader, John F. Kennedy, in the Austrian capital of Vienna. But at Vienna, as at Paris the year before, no progress was made. Both sides stuck adamantly to their positions. Khrushchev issued yet another ultimatum to the West: Allied troops must be withdrawn from Berlin by the end of the year.

Kennedy later stated the Western position: "We do not want to fight, but we have fought before. . . . We cannot and will not permit the Communists to drive us out of Berlin, either gradually or by force."[4] Khrushchev responded by accusing NATO and the West of threatening to unleash nuclear war. If they followed through on this threat, he said, the Soviet side would ultimately emerge victorious and would "bury" the West.

Meanwhile, within East Berlin, living conditions continued to decline. There was a severe lack of adequate housing, as well as shortages of food and many consumer items. During the first six months of 1961, more than 100,000 additional East Berliners left the GDR for good.

The Communist side could no longer just look the other way while thousands upon thousands of East Germans fled the country. Throughout the summer of 1961, there were signs that something was about to happen. Ulbricht stepped up his attacks on "subversives" from the West who, he said, were making their way into East Berlin to undermine the socialist system. The East German government announced that it had recruited 45,000 citizens from the general population to assist the police force and the border guards. The Germans stationed at the border between East and West Berlin were replaced by Soviet troops, armed with automatic weapons.

At 15 minutes after midnight on August 13, 1961, the East German Communists made their move. Party leader Ulbricht gave the orders. They were carried out by his trusted lieutenant, Erich Honecker, the chief of the GDR's ministry of security. Honecker would oversee a course of action none in the West had even imagined possible. He would act as foreman for the construction of a massive concrete wall through the heart of Berlin. The East German government had decided, in effect, to seal in its own people.

Within hours, inner-city trains and bus lines came to a halt. Telephone service to the outside world was cut off. Electricity along the border with West Berlin was shut down. Roadblocks were set up on all major avenues. Thousands of heavily armed militia men filled the streets. Thousands of Soviet troops, backed by East German reinforcements, circled the city. Machine guns appeared atop all major government buildings and in front of the Soviet embassy. At the border there were machine guns as well, including on top of the Brandenburg Gate, the chief crossing point between East and West. Armed soldiers were also stationed every few yards along the border, with rifles drawn and bayonets fixed. The soldiers, like the machine guns, were not facing away from East Berlin, to guard against invasion or interference from the West. They were, rather, faced inward, toward the city they sought to "protect" from the outside world. The heavily armed soldiers stood facing the people of East Berlin.

First, soldiers and laborers worked together to break through the asphalt with jackhammers. Then holes were dug, into which heavy concrete poles were placed. Across the poles, the workers carefully hung barbed wire. Another shift then labored through the night and into the next day to erect a temporary wall of narrow boards and plasterboard, just a few feet behind the barbed wire. In some areas of the city, workers had already started construction of a more permanent structure—a large concrete wall. This would become the notorious Berlin Wall, perhaps the most loathed structure on the face of the earth. The Wall was, when completed, nearly 100 miles

As West Berliners watch, East German laborers build the Berlin Wall.

long. It extended 28 miles through the heart of the city, and then 70 more miles around it—to separate West Berlin from the rest of the GDR. At its tallest point, it was 12 feet high; at its shortest, 9—too tall anywhere to be readily scaled. Built alongside of it were 193 watchtowers and 208 bunkers. Eventually the ugly, bare concrete wall was painted white, but certainly not because the East German authorities worried about its attractiveness. Rather, the white background made it easier for East German border guards, who were armed and had orders to shoot to kill, to see the outline of anyone who might try to scale the wall and escape from the so-called German *Democratic* Republic.

chapter 4

East and West: Separate and Unequal

East Berliners woke on the morning of August 13, 1961, to find that a wall now separated them from the West. Still, the atmosphere in the city remained calm and quiet. The few East Berliners who tried to cross into the West that day were turned away by armed border patrols. Small groups of curiosity seekers gathered at several points along the Wall. Although some may have spoken quietly to themselves about their dismay at the sad turn of events, the machine guns pointed toward them ruled out more vocal protests.

In West Berlin, however, the chief reaction was anger. Large crowds at the Wall jeered the East German border guards a few yards away. Some young West Berliners started tearing at the barbed wire with their bare hands. A few others threw rocks at the East German troops. Eventually, units of the West German police arrived to control the crowd and prevent it from rushing directly toward the eastern barriers.

Tension ran very high. Leaders on both sides appealed for support. A few days after the Wall went up, Walter Ulbricht addressed the people of East Germany. He said that he still held out his hand in friendship to "our dear brothers and sisters, the West German people." But, he explained, the government of the GDR had had to erect the Wall to guard against attempts to overthrow the East German government from the West—from the "Fascists, Nazis, militarists, . . . warmongers, slave traders, and headhunters" who now controlled the government of West Germany.[1] From that day forward, in East Germany the Berlin Wall would be known as the "Anti-Fascist Defensive Wall."

On the same day, Willy Brandt, the mayor of West Berlin, delivered an emotional address from the balcony of the Berlin city hall. In his speech he described the concrete posts from which the Communists had hung barbed wire as spikes sunk in the heart of Germany. All Germans felt the pain, Brandt declared, and all free people must see the wall of shame that the Communists had built—like an ugly scar across the face of the city. Words of support were appreciated, Brandt concluded, but much more was needed. He urged the leaders of the free world to come to Berlin to demonstrate their support for his beleaguered people.

The Western Allies, however, faced a difficult dilemma. As preparations were being made for the building of the Wall, the Soviet leader Khrushchev had predicted the West's reaction: "They will stand there like dumb sheep."[2] This prediction was, in the main, accurate. Many believed that Britain, France, and the United States, as the three guarantors of Berlin's security, had every right to intervene to stop the construction of a permanent barrier dividing the city. However, to do so might provoke an armed attack by the Soviets against Allied troops stationed in West Berlin. The Western Allies, connected to Berlin by only a narrow 110-mile corridor through the Communist GDR, would be hard pressed to respond to such an attack effectively. Some also feared that the military escalation of the Berlin crisis might even lead to nuclear war.

The West limited its support for Berlin largely to moral encouragement. U.S. Vice President Lyndon B. Johnson flew in to greet the 1,500 additional American troops sent to Berlin to strengthen the U.S. military post. The troops marched through the center of West Berlin, led by General Lucius Clay, the American military commander who had coordinated the heroic airlift that had broken the 1948-49 blockade.

German police gaze at President John F. Kennedy as he views the
Berlin Wall from a specially-erected platform in June 1963.

In June 1963, President John F. Kennedy came to Berlin.
Accompanied by Mayor Brandt and other German leaders, he
toured the city and viewed the hideous Wall for himself.
Hundreds of thousands of Berliners lined the streets to greet
Kennedy. The Communist officials in the East had ordered the
Brandenburg Gate—the main opening through the Wall—hung
with red cloth to prevent East Berliners from catching a glimpse
of the American president.

As the hour of Kennedy's speech to the people of West
Berlin drew near, perhaps a million Berliners filled the plaza
in front of the city hall. Defiantly and boldly, John F. Kennedy

spoke of what Berlin had come to mean to free people the world over:

> *There are many people in the world who really don't understand, or say they don't, what is the great issue between the free world and the Communist world. Let them come to Berlin. There are some who say that communism is the wave of the future. Let them come to Berlin. And there are some who say in Europe and elsewhere that we can work with the Communists. Let them come to Berlin. And there are even a few who say that it is true that communism is an evil system, but it permits us to make economic progress.* Lasst sie nach Berlin kommen. *Let them come to Berlin.*[3]

Kennedy then paid tribute to the determination of the brave people of Berlin, who had remained hopeful in spite of the countless difficulties they had been forced to face since the end of the Second World War. Until the Wall was torn down, and Berlin—and Germany—were reunited, Kennedy concluded, the freedom of the people of the world would not be complete. All free people, wherever they lived, Kennedy said, were truly citizens of Berlin:

> *And therefore, as a free man, I take pride in the words* Ich bin ein Berliner *[I am a Berliner].*[4]

The assembled crowd erupted in a tumultuous roar as the American leader addressed them in their native language. Kennedy had shown clearly that the democratic nations of the West still stood firmly behind the beleaguered people of Berlin. Some months later, following John F. Kennedy's assassination, the square in front of West Berlin's city hall would be renamed John F. Kennedy Square, in tribute to the American president who had stood by Berlin in its hour of need.

▼ ▲ ▼

The Wall continued to stand, however. On August 13, 1965, gatherings were held in both East and West Berlin to mark the fourth anniversary of the Wall's construction. In the East, Communist leader Walter Ulbricht and representatives from the Soviet Union and other Communist-ruled "people's democracies" of Eastern Europe made speeches about the new era of "scientific and technological revolution" that beckoned for the GDR. In the West, there were speeches, too—followed by a full hour of silence, during which the people of West Berlin remembered those who had lost their lives attempting to break through the Wall and gain freedom in the West.

The Wall had not stopped 16,500 East Berliners from escaping to the West between 1961 and 1963. Over 600 men, women, and children were fired upon by East German border guards as they attempted to flee, and 68 people were killed.

The methods the East German escapees employed were often quite daring and imaginative. In the early days, when the barrier was little more than barbed wire and plasterboard, some had attempted simply to drive right through, braving a hail of gunfire from the East. When work on the final concrete wall was completed, this method became impossible, and more ingenuity was called for.

Some tried to scale the Wall by throwing a looped rope over to the western side where it might catch onto something solid or be caught and held by someone waiting there. When this method proved successful in several cases, the East Berlin authorities responded by banning the sale of any grade of rope strong enough to hold a human being!

Others attempted to make their way to the other side by following a dark, dirty route through Berlin's ancient sewer system. When the East German police discovered that this was being done, they immediately cemented shut all manhole covers in their part of the city.

An example of a tunnel dug under the Berlin Wall. This tunnel leads from an East Berlin basement *(right)*, under the Wall, and into a West Berlin basement *(left)* in the French sector.

Two families built their own hot-air balloon to use to escape to the West. One afternoon, after two unsuccessful attempts, the group took advantage of favorable wind and weather conditions and glided to freedom, high above the range of the border guards' weapons.

Others dug tunnels under the Wall. Twenty-eight people escaped by means of one of the largest, which was later discovered and sealed by the East Berlin border guards. Max Thomas, 81 years old, led a dozen of his friends, many of them older citizens like himself, to freedom through a tunnel that started behind the chicken coop in his backyard. Another group dug a tunnel to the West that started inside a large burial crypt in an East Berlin cemetery. The escapees would enter the mausoleum

posed as mourners coming to pay their respects to dead rela-
tives. Once inside the crypt, they never reemerged. Instead,
they followed a tunnel that had been dug under the cemetery
grounds to the West! Soon, for every tunnel that had been discovered and closed by the border guards, another was being dug
elsewhere along the Wall.

Other brave Berliners attempted to swim across the city's
canals and rivers, some of which had banks on both sides of the
closely guarded border. Other East Germans tried to swim the
Havel River from elsewhere in the GDR into West Berlin.
Although some managed to avoid the border patrols, others were
not as fortunate. Within a few years, the banks of the Havel
were lined with more than 70 crosses, commemorating those who
had died attempting to flee in this way.

▼ ▲ ▼

As the years passed, the gap between East and West continued
to widen. Chancellor Adenauer and the Christian Democrats
made the economic rebuilding of West Germany their chief priority. Soon, West Germany had developed into one of Europe's
economic powerhouses. Within a generation, the FRG had the
largest trade surplus of any of the world's nations. West
Germans would also soon come to boast the highest per capita
concentration of automobiles, the highest hourly wage, the
shortest work week, and one of the highest standards of living in
the world. Between 1950 and 1980, the average monthly income
for a West German family increased tenfold, and many families
were able to enjoy the fruits of the country's prosperity. Some
had enough money to go on vacations, and even to buy an extra
home in the country. Stores were filled with the latest household
conveniences and fashions. Resort hotels and fancy restaurants
attracted large crowds.

In the East, however, life was not as comfortable. The GDR's
lack of political freedom was matched by its lack of material

comforts. The Communist government emphasized the development of heavy industry, as well as science and technology. Little effort was spent on manufacturing goods to benefit East German consumers. Shoppers were forced to wait in line in state-run shops for long periods of time to buy the few goods that were available, and quality was often poor as well. Stories of the poor quality of consumer goods in the GDR—for instance, of razor blades that wore out after one shave, of shoes that fell apart soon after being put on, and of soap and shampoo that did not lather—soon became very common.

As the decade of the 1970s arrived, the two Germanys seemed firmly positioned on their separate political roads as well. Berlin's former mayor, Willy Brandt, led the Social Democrats to victory in the West German elections of 1969, bringing to an end more than two decades of Christian Democratic control.

Brandt moved quickly to improve relations between East and West. His policies were given the name *Ostpolitik* (East politics). Brandt hoped that reconciliation between East and West might eventually bring about the reunification of Germany. In 1970, the Federal Republic and the USSR signed a treaty renouncing the use of force. The next year, Willy Brandt received the Nobel Peace Prize in recognition of his work as an advocate of political freedom and reconciliation.

Initially the East German leadership resisted Brandt's attempts at closer relations. However, the period of *Ostpolitik* coincided with the policy of closer relations, or détente, being pursued by the governments of the United States and the Soviet Union. When the Soviets attempted to pressure East German Communist leader Ulbricht into accepting Brandt's entreaties, he hedged at cooperating. In 1971, at the insistence of Moscow, Ulbricht was removed as general secretary of the SED. His successor was his former aide, Erich Honecker, the same man who had, ten years before, supervised the construction of the Berlin Wall. Honecker moved quickly to cooperate with Brandt and the West German government.

In 1971, too, the four occupying powers—the United States, the Soviet Union, Great Britain, and France—signed the Four Powers Agreement, which effectively brought a generation's uncertainty over the question of Berlin to an end. The agreement guaranteed the existence of two separate, sovereign German states, joined to one another by a common history and a shared hope of eventual reunification. The Four Powers Agreement also reiterated that West Berlin was part of the territory of the Federal Republic and guaranteed the West access to its portion of Berlin.

A year later, in December 1972, the governments of East and West Germany themselves signed a treaty under which each country accepted the right of the other to exist. In spite of opposition from the Christian Democrats, the treaty was ratified by the West German Bundestag in May 1973. In September of the same year, both the GDR and the FRG were accepted as full members of the United Nations, and both countries established full diplomatic relations with most major governments. The reality of two Germanys now seemed an accepted fact in international politics.

Improved relations at the government level also meant that ordinary German men and women on both sides of the border could visit each other more easily. Travel restrictions were eased. Families were reunited. Schools sponsored student exchanges. In 1971, direct telephone service between East and West Berlin was restored. By the mid-1980s, trade between the two German states had grown to 16 billion deutsche marks.

At first, many thought that Erich Honecker would bring about important reforms within the GDR. To deal with the country's severe housing shortage, construction plans were stepped up. Government pensions were increased, as was financial assistance to families with young children. Steps were taken to build the supply of consumer goods, and the salaries of most workers rose as well. Greater political expression was allowed, and an agreement was reached giving more freedom to the Protestant Church.

▼ ▲ ▼

In time, however, tensions began to develop once again in the relationship between the two Germanys. Following the Soviet Union's invasion of Afghanistan in 1980, relations between the United States and the USSR deteriorated, and the era of détente ended. The Soviets began to station SS-20 mobile missiles in East Germany and Czechoslovakia. In response, the American government announced that intermediate-range Pershing and cruise missiles would be stationed in West Germany.

The Christian Democratic government of Chancellor Helmut Kohl, which had come to power in 1982, agreed to the position-

Young people dressed as skeletons protest the stationing of U.S. nuclear missiles in West Germany.

ing of American missiles in West Germany. However, many West Germans believed that the deployment represented a dangerous militarization of their country. They feared West Germany might even be attacked by the Soviet Union. A new political party, the Greens, which had been formed in 1980, actively opposed the stationing of nuclear weapons on German soil and pushed for stronger laws to protect the environment. Soon massive demonstrations against the Pershing and cruise missiles filled the streets of major West German cities. In 1983, in protest of the American actions, the Soviets walked out of the Strategic Arms Reduction Talks (START) in Geneva. Superpower relations seemed to have reached a new low. As the 1980s wore on, however, the political situation in Eastern Europe would change again—radically.

In March 1985, Mikhail Gorbachev succeeded Konstantin Chernenko as general secretary of the Soviet Communist party. Through the twin policies of *glasnost* (openness) and *perestroika* (restructuring), Gorbachev promised "truly radical changes" in the Communist system. Moreover, his energetic and outspoken manner captured the imagination of people the world over. Gorbachev moved quickly to improve relations with the West. In November 1985, the START talks in Geneva opened again after a two-year lull. After discussion, the two sides reached an agreement to reduce their arsenals of intermediate-range missiles by half.

As relations between the superpowers improved, the East German leader Honecker grew distrustful of Gorbachev's new closeness with the Bonn government. Honecker feared that closer relations between the USSR and West Germany might undermine the GDR's "special relationship" with the Soviet Union.

Since the détente period of the 1970s, Honecker had wanted to make a triumphal visit of reconciliation to the Federal Republic. Such a visit, he believed would establish him in the eyes of the world as the clear equal of the West's leaders. While in Bonn, Honecker also hoped to portray himself as Germany's great champion of peace and disarmament. For years, however, the Soviet leadership had not wanted to encourage too much "independence" on Honecker's part and so had discouraged him from traveling to the West.

Honecker hoped that the more liberal Gorbachev might look more favorably on his plans. But Gorbachev too refused to agree to such plans. Honecker was incensed. How dare this young upstart Gorbachev—19 years his junior, in power only a fraction as long—stand in his way? From this point on, according to observers within the leadership of the SED, "Honecker's 'tirades' against Gorbachev became a staple of . . . Politiburo meetings."[5]

Honecker eventually did travel to the Federal Republic, in the fall of 1987. There, he was greeted warmly by representatives of almost all the major West German political parties. Only the Greens refused to meet with Honecker, both because the party maintained close ties with Honecker's opponents within the GDR and because many Greens resented the East Germans' attempts to take control of the antinuclear movement. Still, Honecker's trip was, from his standpoint, a success. Some leading Social Democrats even began to say publicly that the time had come to abandon the "old fashioned" idea of eventual reunification and deal with the GDR as a full, equal partner.

But Honecker's differences with Gorbachev seemed wider than ever. The Soviet leader had stated on numerous occasions that the Soviet Union would no longer interfere in East Germany's internal affairs. Honecker decided to take Gorbachev at his word. The time was ripe, Honecker thought, to strengthen his position further by moving against the various dissidents—human rights protesters, advocates of religious freedom, would-be emigrants to the West—who had troubled his rule from time to time.

Early in 1988, East German police launched a raid against Berlin's Zion Church, confiscated various publications, and arrested those present. A few months later, several leading East German dissidents dared to march in an officially sanctioned parade carrying a banner that read "Freedom always means

East German leader Erich Honecker (*left*) with West German
Chancellor Helmut Kohl in September 1987

freedom for the dissident." They were immediately arrested,
charged with treason, and ordered to leave the country. In the
early summer of 1988, several hundred rock-and-roll fans
gathered near the Berlin Wall in hopes of hearing music from a
concert taking place a short distance away in the West. Without
warning, the police moved against them with nightsticks and tear
gas. Several hundred were injured.

Late in October of the same year, a member of the East
German Politburo told a foreign journalist that there would
never be an East German version of *perestroika*. Instead of
perestroika, Honecker pursued a policy of *Abgrenzung*, or
"insulation." In Honecker's view, East Germans had to be protected from too much "Westernization" so that they could continue to develop socialism in their own way. Honecker and the
other East German Communist leaders grew so fearful of the
Soviet's changing attitudes that East German authorities even
started to ban the sale of newspapers and magazines from the

Soviet Union in their country. While men and women in capitalist West Germany could freely buy copies of Russian newspapers and magazines, their counterparts in Communist East Germany now faced stiff fines, even imprisonment, if they were caught trying to purchase recent editions of *Pravda*, *Sputnik*, and *Moscow News*, which were smuggled into East Germany from the USSR.

To some observers it seemed as though the GDR's clock was being turned back to an earlier, more severe time. Certainly, Honecker's grip was as tight as ever, and he seemed intent on tightening it further. Perhaps the most ominous sign of this was the news as 1988 drew to a close that East German border guards were once again being ordered to shoot to kill anyone who attempted to flee over the Wall to the West.

chapter 5

The Wall Falls

For more than a century, Hungary's Lake Balaton had been a popular vacation destination for countless Germans, and it remained so even after the establishment of the two Germanys. Communist authorities in the GDR had no qualms at all about allowing East German citizens to travel south across Czechoslovakia, which was also a Communist country, into Hungary to take advantage of Balaton's well-developed and inexpensive tourist facilities.

During the spring and summer of 1989, however, a tide of political reform swept over Hungary. A new reform government intent on following Gorbachev was in power, and opposition groups were being allowed to speak out publicly. On May 2, 1989, the Hungarian foreign ministry announced that it was preparing to remove all fortifications along Hungary's western border with Austria. Within hours, Hungarian soldiers with wire cutters and pliers were dismantling the barbed-wire fences along more than 100 miles of the once heavily guarded "iron curtain."

Almost immediately, many vacationing East Germans grasped the opportunity that lay before them. Scores of the vacationers quickly made their way west from Lake Balaton to the foothills of the Alps along the Hungarian-Austrian border. Carefully avoiding the few troops who still patrolled the frontier, they streamed across the border into Austria. From there, they made their way to the West German embassy in the Austrian capital, Vienna.

As the time for summer vacations arrived, thousands of East Germans began secretly planning to escape to the West by way of Hungary. As in years gone by, they would board special tourist trains for Balaton or drive their small two-cylinder Trabant autos across Czechoslovakia and into Hungary. However, this summer many had no intention of returning to East Germany when their vacations were over. Instead, they too would head for Austria and freedom in the West.

In past years the Hungarian government had taken care to ensure that all foreign visitors returned to their homes at the proper time. Now, however, the Hungarian Communists had become too preoccupied with their own political survival—and too interested in reaching out to the democratic countries of Western Europe—to worry any longer about helping the hard-line government of East German leader Erich Honecker continue to confine its people. Hungarian police no longer stopped East Germans as they walked into the West German embassy in Budapest. The Hungarian government even established several refugee camps to provide food and accommodations for East Germans who refused to return home. Thousands of Germans now camped all across Hungary, patiently awaiting permission from the Hungarian authorities to leave for Austria or West Germany.

At the end of August, Hungarian Foreign Minister Gyula Horn flew to East Berlin to consult with his East German counterpart, Oscar Fischer. Fischer demanded that Hungary carry out its 1969 agreement with the GDR to return forcibly any East Germans attempting to cross into Austria. Horn listened patiently to Fischer but then informed him that although the leaders of the Hungarian government wanted to maintain good relations with their fellow Communists in East Germany, they now felt obligated to carry out the terms of the United Nations convention requiring the free passage of refugees. Thus, the Hungarian foreign minister concluded, his country had no choice but to suspend its agreement with the GDR and allow vacationing East German citizens to cross into Austria.

On September 11, Hungary opened its border with Austria, allowing free passage to all who wanted to cross. By the end of the day, about 20,000 East Germans had gone over to the West. Within a few weeks, they would be joined by more than 10,000 others who had spent the entire summer hiding in the homes of Hungarian friends. Something previously unthinkable was now happening: The Communist government of Hungary was assisting the citizens of another Communist state to flee to the West.

Immediately, Honecker's government in Berlin responded by banning all travel by East Germans to Hungary. But those intent on gaining freedom would not be stopped. Unable to pass into Hungary, large crowds of East Germans began storming into the West German Embassy in Prague, Czechoslovakia, demanding political asylum in the West. As thousands of East Germans crowded into the embassies, living conditions steadily worsened. The embassies simply were not equipped to shelter and feed such large numbers of refugees. Reluctantly, Honecker agreed to grant East Germans permission to leave the country. But he attached a condition: The refugees would not be allowed to pass directly from Czechoslovakia into West Germany. Instead, their trains were to be routed back into the GDR briefly. There, they were to be stripped of their East German citizenship and then "expelled" to the Federal Republic. In this way, Honecker could at least claim that thousands of "undesirables" had been deported from East Germany.

But Honecker's attempt to save face immediately backfired. By not allowing thousands of emigrants to be transported quickly and quietly into West Germany from Czechoslovakia, he created a public spectacle. As three "freedom trains" pulled into the station in the East German city of Dresden, where the refugees were to be officially stripped of their citizenship, a

About 10,000 East German refugees crowd the street outside the West German embassy in Prague, Czechoslovakia, demanding political asylum in West Germany. They were later allowed to board buses that took them to "freedom trains."

crowd of several thousand bystanders rushed forward and attempted to jump aboard. The brutal response of the police stopped all but a few from mounting the platform. Nevertheless an almost identical scene was repeated when the train arrived at Karl-Marx-Stadt several hours later. When the trains finally crossed the border into the Federal Republic, those on board found the route lined with thousands of West Germans who were cheering, waving and shouting words of encouragement to their fellow Germans.

By the end of the summer of 1989, almost 50,000 East Germans had left for the West. One observer estimated that over 2 million East Germans (out of the country's total population of 16.5 million) would move to West Germany if they had the chance. Among those who left—or who wanted to leave—were some of the most valuable members of East German society: doctors, teachers, scientists, technicians, and professionals who had grown weary of the bleak life they lived under the Communist system. In fact, disillusion with the situation in East Germany had become so widespread that one popular joke in the country during the summer of 1989 ended with the line "East Germany— would the last person out please turn off the lights?"

Still, Honecker persisted in making plans for a grand celebration to commemorate the fortieth anniversary of the founding of the Communist GDR. There were to be parades and parties and political speeches. Soviet leader Mikhail Gorbachev had been invited as the guest of honor. He arrived in East Berlin on October 6, the day before the grand celebration was to take place.

Thousands gathered in the streets of the German capital to hail Gorbachev as the great reformer of the socialist system. Banners quoting Honecker himself waved in the breeze. Years before, the East German leader had declared: "To learn from the Soviet Union is to learn how to win!" Now, in a very different era, thousands of East Germans were demanding that their leaders once again follow the Soviet example and initiate *perestroika*-like reform in East Germany.

The next day, Honecker and Gorbachev appeared in Berlin, arms linked in friendship, in celebration of the GDR's anniversary. But deep differences still existed between the two Communist leaders. In private talks with Honecker, Gorbachev reiterated that under no circumstances would he allow Soviet troops to be sent to East Germany to defend Honecker's hard-line position. Yet the East German leader remained unmoved. Honecker had dedicated his life to the East German Communist system and was not about to abandon it now. As long as he was in power, Honecker told Gorbachev, East Germany would remain true to the ways of Marxism-Leninism, whether government policy was defended by the Soviets or not.

In his speech before the East German people the next day, Gorbachev insisted openly that political systems needed to change with the times. When he forcefully warned that "life itself punishes those who delay,"[1] few doubted that he had his East German hosts in mind. At the conclusion of the anniversary festivities, Honecker accompanied his guest to the airport. The two men embraced before Gorbachev boarded the plane for Moscow. Then, as the Soviet leader climbed the steps to his plane, Erich Honecker stood alone at the bottom of the stairs.

Gorbachev and Honecker together in East Berlin

▼ ▲ ▼

Gorbachev's visit was like a spark that set East Germany ablaze. The Soviet leader was barely out of the country when demonstrations against the Honecker regime erupted in various cities across East Germany. On the evening of October 9, thousands marched in the southern city of Leipzig, under the leadership of a recently established reform group, New Forum. Every night for a week, the demonstrations continued. Every night they were met by riot police with tear gas. But now the East German people were no longer frightened of those who had terrorized them for so many years. Every night the crowd demanding political reform, the right to travel freely, and an end to Honecker's rule seemed to grow larger. By October 16, it numbered more than 100,000 people.

Honecker declared that he would never negotiate with those who had "trampled on the moral values of socialism." Furthermore, he said, there would be "no tears shed" over those who had chosen to flee to the West.[2] Honecker decided to put an end to the counterrevolution once and for all. According to secret police documents that later became public, Honecker and Erich Mielke, chief of the security police, were laying plans for a grand scheme to arrest 13,681 East German "dissidents" and imprison them in labor camps throughout the GDR. In addition, more than 70,000 other East Germans were to be placed under constant police surveillance. On October 8, Mielke ordered the Stasi to prepare for "Day X"— the day on which the arrests would be made. However, the massive demonstrations filling the streets by that time made implementation of the plan impossible.

On October 17, according to some reports, Honecker ordered the Leipzig police to arm themselves with live ammunition and to open fire if need be to disperse the demonstration planned in that city that evening. Horrified by the thought of the bloodbath that might take place, the GDR's chief of security, Egon Krenz, flew immediately to Leipzig and personally canceled Honecker's order.

That night, over 120,000 peaceful demonstrators marched through the streets of Leipzig, unhampered by the police for the first time.

Now, even Honecker's own comrades within the Socialist Unity Party turned on their longtime leader. The next day the central committee of the party forced Honecker to resign from office and named Egon Krenz to replace him as leader of the East German party, state, and armed forces. Krenz was the youngest member of the ruling Politburo; at the age of 51, he was a full 25 years younger than Honecker. Many Communists hoped that Krenz would be better able to respond quickly to the challenges the country now faced.

Immediately after assuming office, Krenz appeared on East German television, joking and smiling broadly—in sharp contrast to the stiff, formal manner in which Honecker had always appeared. "My motto remains work, work, work, and more work," he told his discontented fellow citizens, "but work that should be pleasant and serve all the people."[3]

But the people of East Germany were skeptical about the "new Krenz" who was supposedly appearing before them. Few believed that this man who had worked his way up through the Communist Party as one of Honecker's most dedicated lieutenants could actually be a true reformer. They remembered too clearly his years as chief of the Stasi, the much-hated secret police, to trust him completely.

The tide of East Germans leaving for the West showed no signs of decreasing. On November 4 the Communist government of Czechoslovakia announced that it too was opening its borders to all East Germans who wanted to cross into West Germany. Within hours the lines of East German autos at Schirnding on the Czech-German border stretched for more than 14 miles. Within a few days, 50,000 more East Germans had entered West Germany by way of Czechoslovakia.

Massive demonstrations—up to half a million people or more—soon filled the streets of East Berlin. All attempts by Krenz to reach a compromise were quickly rebuffed. Following the government's proposals for changes in the country's law on travel, for example, even more men and women took to the streets of the East German capital. On November 7 the East German cabinet resigned, and Hans Modrow, the popular reform-minded mayor of Dresden, was named as the new prime minister. But even the appointment of the man once praised as "East Germany's Gorbachev" failed to stop the protests. Eventually a million East Berliners were demonstrating openly against their government.

Two days later, on November 9, Günter Schabowski, head of the GDR's ministry of press and information, held a news conference to report on a meeting of the Communist Party Politburo. Schabowski answered a few questions from reporters and then told them that he had one more statement to make. In a matter-of-fact voice, Schabowski announced that, starting immediately, citizens of the German Democratic Republic who wanted to would be allowed to leave the country any time they wished. There would no longer be any need to slip out by way of Hungary, Austria, or Czechoslovakia. East Germans could now pass to the Federal Republic directly through East German crossing points. All they needed was to obtain an exit permit, which would be granted at the borders to anyone who requested one.

All at once, it seemed, the East German Communists had surrendered. The hated Berlin Wall—the major symbol of the entire Cold War between East and West—was now all but irrelevant. If East Germans could travel freely to the West, if they could even leave the country for good if they desired, then what use was the Wall? For many East Germans, who had lived in the shadow of the Wall for almost 30 years, and who had lived under the oppression of the Communist system for more than 40, the news was like a dream come true.

That night the center of Berlin had the atmosphere of a giant party as *Ossis* and *Wessis* (East and West Berliners) danced together atop the Wall. Some West German youths even climbed over to the other side to shake hands or present flowers to the East German border guards. The guards, who until the day before had been ordered to shoot to kill anyone who dared to approach the Wall, shook their heads in amazement at the wondrous turn of events. As one man from East Berlin watched a Westerner chip away pieces of the Wall for a souvenir, he jokingly called out to him: "Put that back! The Wall belongs to us!"[4]

The next day the East German government declared a holiday, and hundreds of thousands of East Berliners flocked to the West. There were massive traffic jams as long lines of small East German Trabants slowly made their way under the Brandenburg Gate, at the heart of the divided city, and through a newly created hole in the Wall. Subway lines connecting the two parts of the city were jammed for hours, and government officials announced that a shuttle bus service was to be established to ease the congestion. Soon the East German government sent work crews to bulldoze five additional openings in the Wall.

Of the multitude of East Berliners who traveled West once the Wall was opened, relatively few decided to remain there permanently. Almost all intended to return to their homes in the East later the same day. The first stop on the Western side was usually a government bank. There, each East German could collect 100 deutsche marks (the equivalent of about $55 at the time) in "welcome money" offered by the government of the Federal Republic. Then, many of the Eastern visitors would find their way to the fashionable Kurfurstendamm (or Ku-damm) shopping district in the center of West Berlin, where they would gaze longingly at the many beautiful but expensive goods for sale in the glamorous boutiques that lined the way. Almost everywhere they went, the East Berliners were greeted warmly. One West Berliner offered free champagne to all those who crossed.

German youngsters help each other to climb up the Berlin Wall as they celebrate the opening of the border.

Restaurants gave out coupons for free meals. There were also offers of free movie tickets or guided tours of West Berlin. A popular Berlin soccer team offered the visiting Easterners 10,000 free tickets to an upcoming match.

Now that the two Germanys could be compared openly with one another, there was little doubt that living conditions in the West were far superior to those in the East. The Communists were completely discredited. With the collapse of the Berlin Wall, German reunification—an idea all but ignored and seemingly forgotten by both sides for so many years—became a real possibility once again.

chapter 6

"We're Not Your Friends"

Overnight the Berlin Wall had become irrelevant. The once mighty psychological and physical barrier that had divided East from West for so many years now held no power over the people of the GDR. Suddenly, it seemed, the whole country was caught up in an irresistible whirlwind of change.

Classes were canceled in East Germany the day after the opening of the Wall, a Saturday. School officials realized that many students, and teachers, would be absent that day, visiting the once-forbidden West. One student in Karl-Marx-Stadt rushed home after school the day classes resumed with surprising news. For years, it had been customary in classrooms across the GDR for teachers to begin the day with the greeting "Be prepared," to which students were expected to respond dutifully "Always prepared." But *this* morning, with classes back in session after the most amazing weekend in East Germany's history, the teacher had entered the classroom and said instead, quite matter of factly, "Good morning." And the students had responded, simply, "Good morning" to her!

An entirely new era had begun for the GDR, and the men who had replaced Erich Honecker scrambled to keep up. The East German government was committed to instituting *perestroika*-like reforms now that the most outspoken reformer within the party, Hans Modrow, was now the GDR's prime minister. A

statement released by the Socialist Unity Party's central committee on November 10 declared: "A revolutionary people's movement has brought into motion a process of great change."[1] The
party promised that a new "action plan" for the GDR, which
would offer the country greater democracy, open elections, and
economic reform, would be drafted.

Extreme reformers within the party soon started to oppose
the leadership of party head Egon Krenz openly. When the
party's central committee refused to confirm four of Krenz's
choices for the ruling Politburo, the appointees were forced to
step down. On November 12, nearly 150,000 party members
gathered outside the SED headquarters in East Berlin and
demanded that the pace of reform be speeded up. When Krenz
came outside to speak with them, his calls for patience, unity,
and discipline were greeted with jeers by younger reform
Communists in the crowd.

In localities across East Germany, hard-line party leaders
were being forced out of office in disgrace. At least three even
committed suicide. The leaders of the party's youth organization
and trade union both resigned under pressure, as did the editor
of the party's major newspaper. Thousands of others were abandoning the party. Within a few months, the membership of the
SED fell from 2.3 million to just 700,000. The membership of
the Free German Youth, the Communist organization for young
people, also declined by half, from 2 million to 1 million.

Krenz and other members of the "old guard" were further discredited when reports began appearing in the East German press
about the special community that had been built for them at
Wandlitz, a suburb of Berlin. At Wandlitz, the SED's leaders
enjoyed a comfortable life. Each family occupied a large, well-
furnished home, which was cared for by a maid and housekeeper.
There was a special store that stocked many kinds of imported
products unavailable to the general population, as well as a
gourmet restaurant, swimming pools, a sauna, and a movie theater
that showed the latest Western films (which were, of course,

Egon Krenz speaks to a crowd of East Berliners.

banned elsewhere in the GDR). Compared to the elegance enjoyed by the "rich and famous" in the West—and by many government leaders the world over—conditions at Wandlitz were certainly not luxurious. But many East Germans bitterly resent- ed that they had been forced to work hard and do without any luxuries whatsoever for many years while their socialist leaders had been taking very good care of their own needs.

Soon, Krenz was being greeted with open contempt whenever he appeared in public. A new slogan was being chanted in cities across East Germany: "Egon Krenz, we're not your friends!" Others in the crowds would shout: "Egon raus!" ("Egon, get out!")

Krenz tried desperately to regain the initiative. But reforms that would have been heralded as daring a few years before—or even a few months before—were now ignored. To a people who had caught a glimpse of freedom after more than 40 years of confinement, the party's proposals were just not enough. Many East Germans were now demanding—openly and without fear—the dismantling of the Communist system and reunification with West Germany. The slogan "Wir sind das Volk" ("We are the people"), which had filled the air in Leipzig, Dresden, Berlin, and other major German cities throughout November of 1989, was now, a few weeks later, giving way to a slightly different turn of phrase: "Wir sind ein Volk" ("We are *one* people").

The East German parliament, the Volkskammer, had for years obediently agreed to every proposal put forward by the leaders of the SED. Now the assembly began to assert its independence. Parties allied with the Communists in the SED, the Liberals and the Democratic Farmers, now moved quickly to distance themselves. The Volkskammer convened in special session on November 13, and for the first time in its history, real debate filled its halls. Horst Sindermann, a loyal Communist who had served as speaker for 13 years, was forced to resign, as were 25 other Communist deputies, including Erich Honecker and his wife, Margot.

Leading Communist officials were summoned before the parliament, where they faced severe questioning. For the first time, Finance Minister Ernst Hofner was forced to admit that the country owed billions of deutsche marks to foreign countries. Erich Mielke, who for 32 years had headed the Stasi, the dreaded secret police, was called before the assembly as well. Some deputies hissed when Mielke began his speech to them with the traditional Communist greeting "Comrades." Dumbfounded and confused, Mielke cried out to them: "But I love you all!"[2] Taunting laughter filled the hall. Mielke had been, just a short time before, perhaps the most feared man in all of East Germany. Now, he seemed pitiful and broken, completely out of touch with reality.

The parliament pressed on with its reforms. Censorship of the press was lifted, committees were established to investigate past corruption and abuses of power, and the right to demonstrate against the government was guaranteed. On December 1, 1989, after debating only 15 minutes, the Volkskammer voted to delete all references to the "leading role" of the Socialist Unity Party from the country's constitution.

On November 23, the Politburo of the SED expelled Günter Mittag, Honecker's close friend and advisor, from the party. A commission was also established to investigate accusations against Honecker himself. Krenz and the Politburo then gave in to reformers' demands and agreed to convene a party congress of SED representatives from across the GDR. But in spite of Krenz's attempts to reach out to the reformers in his own party and his declarations that the party congress would herald a great new day of socialism in the GDR, his support continued to decline. Large crowds continued to torment him wherever he went. Wherever he arrived for a meeting, jeering and booing would fill the air as he emerged from his limousine. A large, hostile crowd was even present as Krenz and his family moved out of their house at the Wandlitz compound to a smaller apartment in Berlin.

Finally, on December 6, Krenz admitted that his position was hopeless, and resigned. He was replaced as party leader by Gregor Gysi, a young lawyer who had made a name for himself during the Honecker years defending the civil rights of the government's most outspoken opponents.

The day after Krenz's fall, the government of Prime Minister Hans Modrow began meeting with representatives of various opposition groups. The situation of the GDR was growing increasingly desperate. During November 1989, an additional 130,000 East Germans had emigrated to the West. By December, the total number for the year stood at over 300,000. Industrial production continued to fall. Agriculture was in total confusion. The whole society seemed gripped by a sense of dread and fear of what the future might bring. Perhaps, Modrow believed, a series of "round-table discussions" with those who had *not* fled to the West—those who still believed that the GDR had a future as an independent, democratic, yet socialist state—might yield solutions to the country's problems.

On December 15, more than 2,000 delegates gathered for the long-awaited party congress of the SED. The next day, the delegates voted to rename the Socialist Unity Party the Party of Democratic Socialism. On December 17, the new general secretary, Gregor Gysi, presented the party's new "revolutionary program." "The German Democratic Republic is in the midst of an awakening,"[3] Gysi observed. But unless the reorganized party could convince the people of the GDR that it had learned from past mistakes, there would be no future for democratic socialism in Germany. Gysi explained that the party was willing to share power with all of those who agreed to work in the interest of the East German people. The days of the party's monopoly were over. Free, open elections were scheduled for May of 1990. In the meantime, the new party leader said, all East Germans should support the government of Prime Minister Modrow and work to strengthen the GDR. This was "of life-and-death importance for our country and our citizens," Gysi concluded.[4] The only other choices were the country's ruin or its annexation by capitalist West Germany.

On December 19, Chancellor Helmut Kohl of West Germany traveled to East Berlin to meet with Modrow. On arrival, Kohl received a hero's welcome. Increasingly, East Germans were coming to view unification with the Federal Republic as their country's best hope. As Kohl and Modrow stood together in the pouring rain and officiated over a new opening of the Berlin Wall at the massive Brandenburg Gate, many sensed that the GDR's days might be numbered.

Chancellor Helmut Kohl waves to the crowd as East German Prime Minister Hans Modrow delivers his speech during the opening ceremony for the new border crossing points at the Brandenburg Gate in East Berlin in December 1989.

Modrow was welcomed politely when he made a return trip to Bonn a short while later. He returned to East Berlin with a few words of encouragement but none of the financial aid he had sought. The West Germans had little interest in shoring up a Communist government that seemed about to topple. To head off the country's complete collapse, Modrow agreed to move up the date of East Germany's first free elections from May to March.

▼ ▲ ▼

A wide array of competing political groups soon emerged on the East German scene. Their presence represented quite a change for a country that had been dominated by a single totalitarian party for so many years. At first, many thought that Modrow and Gysi might be able to lead their reformed, renamed party to victory. Gysi crossed the GDR, speaking in schools, factories, and at open-air rallies, and was greeted warmly wherever he went. As a skilled lawyer, he understood how to impress an audience and put forward his arguments forcefully. His sense of humor also seemed quite refreshing after decades of leadership by the strict, severe Honecker. "After 40 years," he told one audience, "it must be possible for us to have vegetable stores that it's a pleasure to go to, and" he added, "more important, to come out of." He then ridiculed the severe shortages that had always faced East German shoppers: "The permanent choice between cabbage and apples just won't do."[5] Democratic socialism could offer the people of East Germany more, Gysi believed.

Others also favored maintaining the independence of the GDR. The three opposition groups that had organized the mass demonstrations that had led to East Germany's November revolution—New Forum, Democracy Now, and the Initiative for Peace and Human Rights—campaigned together as a common political party, Alliance 90. Alliance 90 resisted calls for reunification with West Germany. Rather, its leaders believed, the GDR should remain a separate state, dedicated to the ideals of both socialism and democracy. In economics, Alliance 90 advocated finding a "third way" between rigid state control of Communism and the unregulated capitalism offered by the West.

Other political groups, however, felt no need to defend the continued existence of the GDR. In the view of these parties, socialism had failed completely. For them, unification with the West was the surest solution to the country's problems.

Three conservative groups—the Christian Democratic Union, the German Social Union, and Democratic Reawakening—formed a coalition called Alliance for Germany and allied themselves with West Germany's governing Christian Democrats. In the early months of 1990, Chancellor Kohl himself made numerous trips to East Germany to assist in the conservative coalition's campaign. Alliance for Germany favored the fastest possible road to reunification of Germany. In the meantime the party believed that the GDR's socialist economy should be replaced with a market-oriented one like that in the capitalist West.

Favoring a somewhat more gradual road to reunification was the Social Democratic Party of East Germany, which soon formed an alliance with the Social Democrats in the West. Former West German chancellor Willy Brandt, the hero of the Berlin crisis of the 1960's, became an active campaigner for the Eastern Social Democrats.

Other Western parties, including the Free Democrats and Greens, soon had counterparts in the East, too. Several groups that had cooperated with the Communists during the Honecker era—the Democratic Farmers Party, the Democratic Women's League, and the National Democratic Party—now offered slates of their own candidates. There were several other Communist groups running as well, including the League of Socialist Workers, the Sparticist Labor Party, and the Communist Party, an extreme Stalinist group claiming to be the only "true" Marxist-Leninist party in the GDR. Even the

German Beer Drinkers Union had a place on the ballot for the March elections!

As the elections drew closer, the country's economy weakened, and more scandals from the past were uncovered. The governing Party of Democratic Socialism fell farther and farther behind. Voters also seemed somewhat skeptical about the untested "third way" advocated by Alliance 90. Although many East Germans respected the Alliance's leaders for their boldness and courage in standing up to the Communists in the past, they seemed hesitant to put the future of their country into the hands of the writers, artists, religious leaders, and professors whom Alliance 90 was offering as candidates.

On election day, March 19, 1990, East Germany held free elections for the first time since 1933 and, in the words of one observer, "voted itself out of existence."[6] Over 93 percent of East Germany's voters went to the polls, and 48 percent of them cast their ballots for the pro-Western, pro-unification Alliance for Germany. The Social Democrats received a disappointing 22 percent of the vote, though public opinion polls as late as a week before the elections had predicted their total vote would be somewhere between 30 percent and 50 percent. Alliance 90, the founders of the East German revolution, gained only 3 percent. In the end, the Party of Democratic Socialism of Gysi and Modrow was happy with the 16 percent of the vote it managed to win.

The new Volkskammer would meet for the first time three weeks later. The Alliance for Germany had gained 193 seats in the 400-member assembly and quickly entered into a coalition with the Liberal Party to form a government. The Liberals, who had cooperated with the Communists as part of the former Socialist Unity Party, had won enough votes to secure 21 seats.

On April 7, the new assembly gathered in East Berlin's ornate Palace of the Republic. Lothar Piche was elected as provisional president. Piche, at age 63, was the oldest member of the governing Alliance for Germany. This was a clear sign that leadership in East Germany was passing into the hands of a new generation.

Many East Germans had taken part in demonstrations calling for free elections.

As its first act, the new Volkskammer passed a resolution admitting East Germany's share of responsibility for the Holocaust and asking Israel for forgiveness. While West Germany's leaders had issued such an apology years before, the Communist leaders for the GDR had stubbornly refused to do so. Rather, they had insisted that the Nazis alone were responsible for the horrors of the Second World War. Now, by admitting the evils of Germany's past, the new leaders of the GDR hoped to be able to move confidently into the future.

The Volkskammer then chose Lothar de Maizière, leader of the Christian Democratic Union, the largest partner in the Alliance for Germany, as prime minister. A quiet, unassuming, somewhat shy man, de Maizière, like Gregor Gysi, had served as a defense lawyer in the days of the Honecker regime. He was also an accomplished amateur musician, who often could be found in his office practicing the viola when the Volkskammer was not in session. Now he was to be the first non-Communist prime minister in the GDR's 40 year history.

In his first address to the parliament in April, de Maizière declared that the people of East Germany had spoken clearly. By an overwhelming majority they had proclaimed their willingness to rejoin their brothers and sisters in the West and to form one united German nation. The goal of his government, de Maizière said, would be "to achieve the unity of Germany swiftly and responsibly."[7] No one, including even de Maizière, had any idea just how swiftly German unification would come about.

chapter 7

The Dream Becomes Real

A few days after the fall of the Berlin Wall in November 1989, Chancellor Kohl appeared before the West German Bundestag and presented ten points outlining his views on future relations between the two Germanys. There were many areas in which the FRG and GDR might cooperate, Kohl said—increasing trade, strengthening economic relations, and improving the environment, among others. Eventually, Kohl said, the two states might want to form some kind of loose confederation, and certain government offices might even be combined. At some unspecified time, rather far in the future, Kohl said, the unification of Germany might become a possibility.

When in a later conversation Kohl estimated that German reunification could take perhaps five years, several other European leaders became alarmed. At a European Community summit meeting in December, British prime minister Margaret Thatcher told Kohl forthrightly that German reunification should be delayed at least ten years, until well after the turn of the century. Rapid reunification of Germany, Thatcher feared, might undermine peace and stability in Eastern and Central Europe and might even lead hard-line Communists within the Soviet Union to overthrow Gorbachev. Furthermore, Thatcher declared, in the absence of a formal treaty ending the Second World War, it was ultimately up to the victorious Allies in that conflict, not to the Germans themselves, to determine the pace of German unity.

The French were also alarmed. A nineteenth-century French diplomat had once remarked, "Germany doubled equals France halved," and many French people remembered how a strong, united Germany had attacked France three times since 1870. Since the division of Germany following World War II, relations between France and Germany had never been better. Ancient fears had given way at last to normal, good-neighborly relations. Were Germany to be reunited as the largest and most powerful nation in Europe again, many feared a resurgence of the extreme German nationalism that had cost France dearly over the years.

Most uneasy of all were the Poles. Poland had suffered horribly at the hands of Germany during World War II. Over 6 million Poles, half of them Jews, lost their lives during the war—the highest percentage of any nation. In 1939, Hitler and Stalin had divided Poland between Germany and the USSR. The Yalta Conference at the end of the war had reestablished Poland as an independent country—largely at the expense of the defeated Germans. The new German-Polish border was drawn along the Oder and Neisse rivers, hundreds of miles west of the pre-World War II boundary.

Even though an official treaty ending World War II had never been signed, the Oder-Neisse line had come to be viewed as the permanent border between Poland and Germany. The government of the Federal Republic had long given up claim to Germany's former territories in the east. But Poland feared that should Germany reunite, treaties signed with either West or East Germany might be open to renegotiation, and questions about the border might arise once again. Poland's new non-Communist prime minister, Tadeusz Mazowiecki, demanded that Poland have a place in any Allied talks leading to German reunification. Furthermore, Mazowiecki insisted, Germany must be forbidden from reuniting unless its government signed a formal treaty with Poland, recognizing the Oder-Neisse border.

On December 11, 1989, at the invitation of the Soviet Union, the Allied Command Council met in West Berlin for the first time since 1948. The council was still officially charged with exercising the Allies' postwar rights in Germany. The British, French, and Soviet representatives all expressed reservations about possible reunification. Only the American representative came out completely in favor of the idea.

▽ ▲ ▽

Meanwhile, the internal situation within the GDR continued to unravel. Shortly before the East German elections in March, Prime Minister Modrow had told Chancellor Kohl that the country was in such disarray that when he gave orders, nothing happened. As the GDR's economy continued to stagnate, thousands of East Germans moved to the West each month. The national treasury was nearly bankrupt, with no money to pay for the huge foreign debt, environmental cleanup, and social problems the Communists had left behind.

Kohl decided that the process of reunification must be speeded up, in spite of international objections. "We must get the hay into the barn before the storm," the German chancellor told one of his advisors.[1] The country must be united again before the East German state crashed to the ground and before widespread disorder resulted.

The reluctant Allies eventually realized that rapid German reunification was going ahead whether they supported it or not. In early 1990, Modrow visited Moscow and returned with news that the Soviets would accept the idea of a single Germany—if Germany pledged to remain neutral and withdrew from both NATO and the Warsaw Pact. Kohl lost no time in rejecting the offer: The idea of a united but neutral Germany had first been put forward by Stalin in 1952. Kohl and the Western Allies agreed that a united Germany must remain part of NATO—an idea that Soviet leader Gorbachev seemed adamant in refusing to accept.

Attempts were made to reach a compromise. The West German foreign minister Hans-Dietrich Genscher drew up a slightly different plan: Germany would remain part of NATO, but after reunification, NATO troops would not be stationed in the territory of the former GDR. Furthermore, Genscher added, the Soviet Union would be given an interim period of several years to remove its troops from German soil.

On February 1, Genscher flew to Washington, D.C., to present his plan to President George Bush. There, representatives of the U.S. State Department gained his acceptance of a frame-

During a visit to Washington in 1989, West German Foreign Minister Hans-Dietrich Genscher (*right*) had presented George Bush with a piece of the Berlin Wall.

work they had developed for reunification. Under this plan, later called the Two Plus Four, East and West Germany would have ultimate responsibility for negotiating the details of reunification. Once these basic details had been worked out, the German representatives would meet with the four Allies to discuss issues of international concern, including future German membership in NATO. Poland would also be consulted when questions of Germany's permanent boundaries were discussed.

The Two Plus Four talks began in May 1990. The Soviets still insisted that limits had to be placed on the role of a reunified Germany within NATO. Gorbachev reiterated his position at a summit conference with President Bush in Washington later that month. Bush, however, insisted that four-power control over Germany would end as soon as unification took place. From that moment on, questions of Germany's foreign policy—including NATO membership—would be decided by the Germans themselves.

Behind the scenes Gorbachev was coming to realize that the Soviets might eventually have to give in and allow Germany to maintain its membership in NATO. One thing he could not now afford, he knew, was a major break with the Allies. He had placed much emphasis on his ability to cultivate close, cooperative relations with the West. Hard-line Communist opponents within the Soviet Union seemed to be growing in strength. To lose a major showdown with the West now would further weaken Gorbachev's position and might even lead to his removal from power.

The two Germanys seemed to grow closer every day. The March electoral victory of Kohl's allies in East Germany had emboldened the chancellor to speed up the pace even more. The first step toward unity, the West German government decided, would be the joining of the countries' currencies and economic systems. In the spring of 1990, the West German state bank, the Bundesbank, announced that as of July 1 the Western deutsche mark would become the official currency both in the East and in

Thousands of East Germans try to enter a bank on the Alexanderplatz in East Berlin at midnight on July 1 to exchange East German ostmarks for West German deutsche marks.

the West. As of that day, East Germans would be able to exchange their ostmarks (as the currency of the GDR was called) for an equal amount of deutsche marks, up to a specified limit. (Above this limit, ostmarks could be exchanged at the rate of two for every deutsche mark—still a very generous rate of exchange given that the ostmark was by this time just about worthless.)

Very early on the morning of July 1, long lines formed outside of banking offices across East Germany. By the middle of that same day, over 3 billion ostmarks had been exchanged. Within a few weeks, the total amount exchanged would reach 17 billion.

The next day, July 2, the East German Volkskammer agreed to schedule the first all-German elections in December. Many shook their heads in amazement at how quickly the day of unification was approaching. As the summer progressed, the pace would quicken even more.

On July 14, West German leaders Kohl and Genscher traveled to Moscow to meet with Gorbachev. At their meeting, both sides summarized the results that had been achieved by the Two Plus Four process up to that time. After unification, Germany would make no claim to territories lost after World War II. Germany would refrain from the development of nuclear, chemical, and biological weapons. NATO would not station nuclear weapons in the territory of the former GDR. The Soviets would have an interim period of several years in which to remove their troops from Germany. Once the country was reunited, the Allies' rights in Germany would end.

Something in the tone of Gorbachev's voice convinced Kohl that the Soviet leader was willing to make even further concessions.

"Then you agree that united Germany will regain full sovereignty?" Kohl asked Gorbachev.

"Of course," Gorbachev responded, adding that NATO troops could be stationed in former GDR territory as long as Soviet troops were allowed to remain there during a transitional period. Then, as though to underscore the point he was making, the Soviet leader repeated: "Germany can remain a member of NATO."

"The breakthrough is here!" a German official wrote in his journal that night. And he labeled the July 15 meeting with Gorbachev "the Miracle of Moscow." Gorbachev had removed the last roadblock to rapid reunification.[2]

Yet the two Germanys still had other issues to discuss before their union became complete. An especially emotional issue was abortion. GDR law allowed women almost unrestricted access to abortions. In the FRG, however, abortions were strictly limited, allowed only in very rare cases. The German representatives to the Two Plus Four negotiations decided to sidestep this difficult subject. The more lenient Eastern law would continue in effect in the lands formerly part of the GDR for two years. During that time the Bundestag would draft a new abortion law for the entire country.

In addition, according to Article 23 of the Basic Law, West Germany's constitution, the states of East Germany would need to be reorganized to be able to apply for admission to the Federal Republic. In July, the East German Volkskammer abolished the 17 counties, or *Bezirke*, into which the Communists had divided the territory of the GDR, and it reinstituted the *Länder* that had existed prior to 1945.

The way was now clear for formal reunification to take place. On August 31, representatives of East and West Germany signed a 1,000-page treaty containing the final details of reunification. October 3, 1990, was set as the date for the momentous event.

On September 13, the final session of the Two Plus Four group met in the ornate ballroom of the Oktyabrskaya Hotel in Moscow. For the last time, too, the four Allied powers met to deal with the question of Germany—a question over which they had argued for nearly half a century and over which they had nearly gone to war several times. One after another, the foreign ministers of Great Britain, France, the United States, the Soviet Union, and East

The signing of the document that officially ended the rights of the Allied powers in Germany. From left to right are James Baker of the United States, Douglas Hurd of Britain, Eduard Shevardnadze of the Soviet Union, Roland Dumas of France, Lothar de Maizière of East Germany, and Hans-Dietrich Genscher of West Germany.

and West Germany affixed their signatures to the document officially ending the rights of the Allied powers in Germany. "Only peace will emanate from German soil," the treaty declared. In a sense, the signing of the Treaty on the Final Settlement with Respect to Germany formally brought World War II to a close.

"We have drawn a line under World War II," Soviet foreign minister Eduard Shevardnadze declared, "and we have started keeping the time of a new age." U.S. Secretary of State James Baker agreed: "Let our legacy be that after 45 years, we finally got the political arithmetic right. Two plus four adds up to one Germany in a Europe whole and free."[3]

Twenty days later, at midnight on October 3, 1990, Germany officially became one nation again. Eleven months before, there had been dancing for joy on top of the Berlin Wall. This night too there would be dancing in the streets. But now there was also a growing understanding of the great challenges that lay ahead.

chapter 8

The High Cost of Unification

On December 2, 1990, Germans on both sides of the former East-West boundary voted in the first all-Germany elections since 1932. Representatives from over 40 political parties stood for office. The result was an overwhelming victory, in East and West alike, for Chancellor Helmut Kohl and the Christian Democrats.

Kohl's governing coalition received more than 55 percent of the votes cast. The leading opposition group, the Social Democrats, received only 33 percent—the worst showing by that party in over 30 years. In the lands of the former East Germany, Alliance 90 received enough votes to gain only a single seat in the new Bundestag, or parliament. The former SED, now Party for Democratic Socialism, would hold only two.

The new Bundestag convened on December 20 in the old Reichstag building in Berlin. One of the first matters to be decided was the location of the country's capital. Many believed that Berlin, always acknowledged by both sides as Germany's official capital, should once again become the seat of the government. Others, however, favored keeping the capital in the smaller western city, Bonn. Much money had been spent over the years in the construction of various government buildings in Bonn. Indeed, construction of a new $151 million parliament building had been begun only in 1986—when few thought that unification was a real possibility. The building itself would not be ready for occupancy until late in 1992. Other large government buildings were still under construction in Bonn as well, and some sources estimated that it would cost $47 billion to move the entire German government to Berlin.

Nevertheless, after a long and emotional debate on the issue, the Bundestag finally decided on Berlin as the new capital. The move of government offices to the east would start in 1998. The entire moving process was to be completed by the year 2000.

Other issues would take even longer to resolve. Many industries in the eastern part of the country were in very poor shape. Erich Honecker and his chief economic advisors had dreamed of transforming East Germany into "the Japan of Eastern Europe"—a world leader in the field of computers and advanced technology. However, though certain areas of technology in the GDR, such as the development of computer software and medical technology, for instance, met world standards, many facets of the economy, especially the production of consumer goods, lagged far behind.

Many of the manufacturing plants of East Germany had become inefficient and outdated under the heavily centralized Communist economic system. There had been no such thing as open competition. In any given industry, a single state-owned company had complete control. If the people in the former GDR had wanted to buy something, they had no choice but to buy East German-produced goods at government-run shops.

Rather than reforming the outmoded, centralized command economy, Honecker had remained dedicated to Communist economic principles. A short time after replacing Walter Ulbricht as East German leader, he moved to centralize business and industry even further. Thousands of small shops and factories that had somehow remained in private hands were taken over by the state. Industries were then grouped together in large government-owned conglomerates, known as *Kombinate*.

East Berliners take a close look at a Mercedes Benz automobile at a West Berlin dealer.

Likewise, the country's farms were all organized into large collectives, in which individual farmers had little decision-making power.

In July 1990 the economies of the two Germanys were merged. The East German market was immediately flooded with all manner of products from the West. In spite of the higher prices many of these goods commanded, East German consumers found them far preferable to the shoddy, dull merchandise they had put up with for over 40 years. Clothing, appliances, and household goods produced in the GDR sat untouched on store shelves while Eastern consumers snapped up Western products.

West German automobiles became increasingly popular. Previously, East Germans had had to wait 10 to 15 years and spend nearly a year's salary to purchase a flimsy, unreliable Trabant automobile. The Trabant, with its two-cylinder engine, cheap fiberglass body, and smoke-belching exhaust system, had become the butt of jokes throughout Europe as well as within the GDR. One commentator described the Trabant as little more than a motorbike with four walls. Now no one, it seemed, wanted to buy a "Trabi"—even when the government car manufacturer drastically slashed its prices.

Faced with competition from the West, one third of all businesses in the former East Germany soon went bankrupt, and many others struggled to survive. After unification, the government of the reunited Federal Republic moved quickly to dismantle the centralized socialist system and replace it with a market-oriented one. A new state agency, the Treuhandanstalt, or Trusteeship, was established to oversee the process of privatization, that is, the transfer of state-owned businesses into private hands.

With the decease of the GDR, the Treuhandanstalt gained control of approximately 12,000 different companies—"everything from beauty parlors to shipyards," in the words of one newspaper report. The same article summed up the Treuhandanstalt's daunting challenge:

> *For Sale: Thousands of eastern*
> *German companies, most in*
> *dilapidated condition with disputed*
> *ownership, dubious management,*
> *outmoded products, vanishing*
> *markets, heavy debts, and thousands*
> *of unnecessary employees.*
> *Everything . . . must go.*[1]

In reality, finding investors to purchase some of the companies was relatively easy. Western businessmen competed with
one another for the purchase of some of the East's more
advanced makers of tools, industrial machinery, and printing
equipment. However, with a few exceptions, most East German
enterprises offered little to entice Western interest or invest-
ment. West Germany's Volkswagen took over the state automobile factory at Sachsenring, the same factory that had produced the much-mocked Trabant. Another large West German
auto manufacturer, Daimler Benz, took over a large truck
plant outside of Berlin. Converting the many Eastern chemical
plants and mining companies, however, to the more stringent
environmental laws of the Federal Republic proved too costly.
It was fiscally more sensible just to close them down. The East
German State Steel Works also failed to thrive in the new economic climate. Inefficiency made its prices three times those of
its competitors in West Germany. The high prices garnered by
state-supported agriculture in the GDR also forced many farm-
ing enterprises in the East out of the market.

The authorities at the Treuhandanstalt moved quickly to
complete the transition to a market economy. Unprofitable
businesses that could not be sold were closed down at the rate
of 10 to 15 per day. All together, 3,000 businesses were
closed. By the fall of 1992, the Treuhandanstalt's work was
completed, and 9,000 businesses in eastern Germany had
been privatized.

While many Germans were confident that the country's
economy would eventually rebound, many others experienced
severe hardship. As unprofitable institutions were closed,
thousands of workers in all sectors of the economy, laborers
and professionals alike, lost their positions. By early 1991,
unemployment in the former GDR rose to nearly 40 percent
of the work force.

Even those who still held jobs worked at salaries that were
on the average only half of those for similar jobs in the West.

And Western capitalism brought with it much higher prices for most goods and services. By 1991, eastern German rents, for instance, were four times higher on average than they had been two years before. Many East Germans began to complain of what they saw as a "conquistador attitude" on the part of Western officials and businesses. To some Western entrepreneurs, the newly acquired eastern *Länder* were little more than colonies to be exploited for monetary gain

▼ ▲ ▼

The people of western Germany also bore part of the cost of reunification. The price tag for unifying East and West was destined to be much higher than Chancellor Kohl and his advisors had believed it would be. All during the months leading to unification, Kohl had consistently maintained that no additional taxes would be needed to pay for unification. Rather, he said, economic growth brought about by opening new markets in the East would generate enough new tax revenue to pay the costs associated with rejoining East and West Germany. This was the platform upon which Kohl and his party campaigned in the elections of March and December 1990. Even before formal reunification, a German Unity Fund worth $70 billion was established to modernize and upgrade facilities in the East. Kohl had maintained that this fund would be sufficient to pay for unification.

But costs soon began to spiral out of control. Western authorities had badly underestimated the poor condition of roads, transportation facilities, schools, and public buildings in the East. Modernizing the East German telephone system alone was a huge task. Ten million miles of copper and fiber-optic cable had to be installed. Two thousand new telephone exchanges had to be built. The number of telephones in the eastern part of the country would nearly quadruple, from 1.8 million in 1989 to 7.1 million by 1997. The final cost of this project alone would be over $30 billion.

The environmental damage caused by 40 years of Communist rule also had to be faced. Shortly after reunification, the German environmental ministry sponsored a study of the situation in the former GDR. Its findings confirmed the sad state of that land's environment:

> *The drinking water of over 60 percent of the people in East Germany was "at times or permanently" unsafe. In some places, drinking water had such a high concentration of harmful substances that pregnant women and infants were told not to drink it and to use bottled water instead.*
>
> *More than 60 percent of communities dumped untreated sewerage directly into rivers and canals.*
>
> *Forty percent of the ground cover was considered spoiled. In some areas the ground was so contaminated by chemicals and toxics that the only way to solve the problem would be to remove the topsoil in trucks.*
>
> *As a result of living in such a poor environment, East Germans had a significantly lower life expectancy than their counterparts in the West. While men in West Germany lived an average of 72 years, East German men had a life expectancy of only 69.5 years. Among women, the difference was even more pronounced: 78.5 years for Western women; only 71.5 years for those in the Eastern part of the country.*[2]

The eastern environment presented a "considerable health threat to the population," according to Environment Minister Klaus Toepfer late in 1990.[3] During that year the government of the Federal Republic spent nearly $100 million cleaning up

During the 40 years of Communist rule, East Germany had suffered severe environmental damage. This photo shows the effects of acid rain on a forest.

the East German environment. But Toepfer admitted that this sum represented just the first payment in what would prove to be a massive, long-term effort that might eventually cost billions of dollars.

The government of the Federal Republic faced other expenses as well. Under the Two Plus Four agreement, the West German government had agreed to pay the costs of withdrawing Soviet troops from East Germany and of building new bases for these troops in the USSR: a total of $7.6 billion in all. Another expense was the guarantee of a monthly income of 550 deutsche

marks (about $350 in 1990) to every German citizen imprisoned
by the Communists for political offenses.

The list of new and unanticipated expenses grew so long
that it soon became apparent that in spite of Chancellor
Kohl's hopes, taxes would have to be raised. Increased trade
within Germany would not be sufficient to cover the new
expenses. By 1992, industrial production in the East had
sunk to barely one third of what it had been before the
Berlin Wall fell. By 1992, too, Germany's economy in general
was in the midst of an economic recession that showed few
signs of improvement.

The German government's costs associated with reunification amounted to $86 billion for the year 1991 alone. In 1992,
that amount rose to over $100 billion. In the years that fol-
lowed, it would rise still higher. Some sources estimated that
by the turn of the century, the total cost of uniting East and
West Germany would amount to well over $1 trillion. In addi-
tion, private companies investing in the East are expected to
spend a similar amount.

To cope with the country's soaring budget deficit,
Chancellor Kohl introduced a "solidarity surcharge" on all
income taxes paid by individuals and corporations. Energy
taxes were to be increased as well, making Germany among the
most expensive places in Europe in which to buy gasoline. In
addition, Kohl announced in 1993 that various government
social programs, including unemployment and welfare benefits
were to be reduced.

Many people, Easterners and Westerners alike, resented
Kohl's policies. They complained that they had not been suffi-
ciently warned of the sacrifices that would be needed to bring
together the two Germanys. The reunification of Germany was
an unprecedented historical event. Never before in history had
such vastly different social and economic systems merged so
rapidly. The costs of unification were indeed immense. But
when the first anniversary of the reunification of their country

came on October 3, 1991, most Germans found reason to celebrate—though not with the same exuberance that had marked other great days in recent German history. Yet most continued to agree that as difficult as the present was, it was far preferable to the bleak and bitter past whose memory haunted them still.

chapter 9

Ghosts from the Past

Once unification had been achieved, Germans from East and West could not simply live happily ever after, as in a fairy tale. The monetary costs of unification would be vast, and the difficulties created by reunification were great as well. Germany's history presented its people with hard questions and painful memories. These issues rose like ghosts out of the past as the reunited Germany attempted to make its way through the closing decade of the twentieth century. The Germans called this difficult, painful process *Vergangenheits bewaltung*—"mastering the past."

In the early winter of 1989, with Honecker out of power and the Communist German Democratic Republic hovering near collapse, many East Germans had demanded to know the full story about the Stasi, the much-hated ministry for state security. In spite of reforms promised by the new government of Prime Minister Hans Modrow and in spite of Modrow's willingness to enter into talks with the opposition, many believed that the Stasi was still exerting an important influence in East Germany. Even after the fall of the Berlin Wall in November 1989, small groups of demonstrators at opposition-sponsored rallies would eye each other suspiciously. Each side suspected that other demonstrators were Stasi agents in disguise! Among the first demands that representatives of New Forum and other opposition groups made in the group discussions known

as the Round Table was for a full accounting of the activities
of the Stasi.

On November 29, Modrow ordered the Stasi to stop all spying
on East Germans and confine its activities to gathering intelligence in other countries. In some areas of the country, Stasi
agents were given jobs driving public buses or government
trucks, to take the place of some of those who had fled to the
West! Modrow also announced a timetable for disbanding the
Stasi completely. A new agency, the Office for National Security
(AfNS), would be established to guard against the rise of neo-
Nazi lawlessness and violence within the GDR.

Many East Germans were skeptical. They sensed that the
AfNS was merely a ploy to keep the Stasi alive under a different
name. Indeed, many members of the opposition changed the
order of letters in the abbreviation of the new security office's
name, referring to it not as the AfNS, but as the "Nasi"
instead—a clear reference both to the Communist Stasi and to
Hitler's Nazis.

When it was discovered that Stasi agents in some parts of the
country had begun to burn and shred files in their offices, many
believed that the time of waiting for the East German government to reform itself was over. Citizens' committees against the
Stasi were formed in seven major East German cities, including
Berlin. In Greifswald, a city on the Baltic coast, a human chain
of 200 men and women surrounded the Stasi headquarters 24
hours a day to stop the carting away of any further documents.

Eventually, two leading members of the Greifswald city government were able to enter the building and seal its 70 filing cabinets
and safes. Around-the-clock shifts of citizens were stationed
inside as well, to keep watch over the activities of the security
agents who remained at their desks. One afternoon, those stationed outside discovered smoke pouring from the building's
chimney. They immediately notified the monitors inside, who
then rushed to the building's basement and saved several huge
sacks of documents from being thrown into the furnace.

Modrow tried to calm the opposition's fears by removing 17 former Stasi officers from the leadership of the AfNS. Honecker's close friend, Erich Mielke, who had headed the Stasi for many years, was arrested and imprisoned. Corruption charges were filed against Honecker and five other members of his Politburo. Then, on December 14, the government gave in to opposition demands and announced that the AfNS too would be dissolved. A few hours later, Modrow announced that two new government security agencies would be formed and that these bodies would have the same names as their counterparts in West Germany: the Federal Intelligence Service and the Office for Protection of the Constitution.

But Modrow continued to resist a full accounting of Stasi activities. Some feared that Modrow, far from being "East Germany's Gorbachev," was actually a hard-line Communist in disguise, seeking to continue Stasi influence under yet another name. On January 8, 1990, the opposition issued an ultimatum to the government: If Modrow did not report the full extent of Stasi influence within one week, the opposition would withdraw from the Round Table meetings. East Germany would be plunged into an even greater political uncertainty.

▼ ▲ ▼

On January 15, Modrow came to the Round Table talks in a conciliatory mood. The establishment of any new security apparatus would be delayed until after the March elections, he promised. He also ordered his chief deputy, Manfred Sauer, to deliver the long-demanded report on the Stasi.

The Stasi had employed 85,000 full-time agents, Sauer said. Of this number, about 50,000 were still on government payrolls. Between 1980 and 1989, the size of the agency had doubled. The sole job of 2,000 agents was to tap telephones, 2,100 were to steam open letters and read other people's mail, and 5,000 followed "suspects" from place to place. The Stasi also boasted an armory that included 200,000 pistols. Even though the average East German had to wait 10 to 15 years to purchase an automobile, the Stasi had a fleet of thousands of cars at its disposal night and day. The agency had complete control over 3,000 telephone lines, in a country where only one in every three homes had its own telephone. While most East Germans waited in line for hours to purchase the meager offerings of government shops, a special network of grocery stores, barbershops, medical offices, and sports facilities had been established for Stasi agents and their families.

If Modrow believed that Sauer's report would calm the fears of the opposition, he was mistaken. Instead, when the citizens of East Germany heard the extent of Stasi abuses, they grew even angrier. On January 15 the leaders of New Forum called for a mass demonstration "against the Stasi and the Nasi." A few hours later at five o'clock in the afternoon of the same day, over 100,000 people gathered outside of Stasi headquarters on Normannen Street in East Berlin.

As one the crowd shouted slogans that had become familiar over the preceding few weeks: "We are the people!" "Down with the SED!" "Never again Stasi." Then the crowd's anger overflowed. One group of protesters scaled a high wall outside the building, shattered the building's glass front door, and streamed inside. Soon, hundreds of others followed them. The headquarters of the loathed security apparatus was now in their hands!

Inside, some smashed furniture and overturned desks. Others scrawled anti-Stasi graffiti everywhere—slogans such as "It stinks in here!" "Spied on long enough—now out!" and, most often, "I WANT MY FILE!" A few even urinated against the walls to show their utter contempt for the hirelings who had spied on their own people. Cabinets were ransacked, files were collected, and, soon, reams of paper were being tossed from windows and down stairwells as the large crowds, both inside and outside the building, continued to cheer wildly.

Using a trowel, an East German demonstrator destroys the glass
entrance door of the Stasi headquarters on January 15, 1990.

Immediately, Prime Minister Modrow drove to Normannen Street and appealed for calm. The leaders of the opposition soon joined him. Once peace was restored, the Round Table negotiations reconvened, and the opposition demanded that the government publish a complete listing of all Stasi facilities and allow individuals access to their own Stasi files.

It took the government of the GDR three weeks to assemble the complete report on the workings of the security apparatus. The facts contained in this more complete report were even more alarming than those Manfred Sauer had supplied several weeks before.

The report confirmed Sauer's account of 85,000 full-time Stasi agents. However, rather than the 109,000 private informers Sauer had reported, it was revealed that between 1 and 2 *million* East Germans had served as agents of the Stasi at one time or another. Stasi agents formed a major part of the country's total population of approximately 16 million. The agents had operated in every aspect of East German society. Their professed goal had been "an espionage network that would cover every citizen in the GDR."

The Stasi left behind archives that filled 125 miles of shelf space—over 2 trillion pages in all, weighing a total of 12.5 million pounds. The Bundestag took a year to decide how the information contained in the Stasi's files should be made public. Deputies were deeply divided—as was the country as a whole— over the issue. Some believed that the files should be opened to all who wanted to see them, with no restrictions whatsoever. Most, however, believed that some restrictions had to be placed on access to the files: There was no way, after all, of guaranteeing whether the information in particular Stasi reports was accurate or not. Still others believed that the sad legacy of the Stasi belonged in the past; the important thing now was for a united Germany to move forward together. Advocates of this viewpoint held that opening the files to public scrutiny would cause undue hardship and pain for the entire nation. These

Germans believed that the files should be destroyed, or at least sealed away for many years.

While the Bundestag debated the issue, Joachim Gauck, a Lutheran minister from Rostock who had helped to organize the opposition in that city, was named custodian of the files. However, in the time between the disbanding of the Stasi and reunification, many files containing sensitive information were stolen from Stasi offices throughout the GDR. Sometimes these files were sold to newspapers and magazines.

The Stasi had infiltrated all facets of East German life. It was shocking to realize that some of Honecker's harshest critics had worked as paid agents of his regime. Manfred Stolpe, one of the highest officials of the Protestant Church in East Germany and leader of the East German wing of the Social Democratic Party, admitted that he had regularly talked to the Stasi for over 25 years. A short while later, Wolfgang Schnur, one of the leaders of the pro-unity Alliance for Germany, admitted that he too had helped the Stasi. Reports also began to link well-known writers and athletes with the activities of the security apparatus.

The greatest shock, however, came just a few weeks after reunification. Reports were published that tied Lothar de Maizière, the only non-Communist prime minister in East Germany's history and a member of Chancellor Kohl's cabinet, to the Stasi. One report that appeared in several German newspapers in December 1990 indicated that de Maizière had been spying on his coworkers for more than 20 years. While de Maizère consistently maintained his innocence, new evidence supporting the original charges was also published. De Maizière had no choice but to resign from the government and return to private life as a lawyer.

▼ ▲ ▼

On November 14, 1991, the Bundestag finally reached an agreement on the files. Under the terms of a new law, individuals would have full access to their own files; others, however, would not be permitted to see them. The press would be allowed to publish information it received about the contents of individuals' files, even if those involved refused to grant their permission. Finally, Wolfgang Schnur was given the power to decide when and whether additional information about Stasi agents and operations was to be released.

Countless lives were changed by the information contained in the Stasi dossiers. Many Germans discovered that they had been spied on over the years by friends, neighbors, and colleagues. Others discovered even more shattering truths. Vera Wollenberger had been one of the Communist government's most outspoken opponents. She had founded Church From Below, a group demanding human rights for all East Germans, and was a leader of the country's independent peace movement. In the first all-German elections in December 1990, she had been elected to the Bundestag and had helped to draft the law allowing citizens to examine their secret police files.

It came as no surprise to Wollenberger that the Stasi had a file on her. She had assumed that the state security forces had been spying on her since the start of her dissident activities nearly 20 years before. When she read her file, she realized that the Stasi had relied mainly on reports from an informer named Donald. These reports not only gave details of Wollenberger's public activities but also contained information about the most intimate aspects of her private life and that of her family. Only one person could have provided the Stasi with such personal information: "Donald" was, in fact, Wollenberger's husband, Knud.

Two other East German human rights activists, Gerd and Ulrike Poppe, also learned that the Stasi had been working against them for more than 20 years. Gerd Poppe was a highly trained physicist, but the Stasi had had him fired from his position. Eventually he had found work as a swimming pool attendant. Later, the security police had introduced an agent named Harald to Ulrike in the hopes that the two might have an affair that would bring the Poppes' marriage to an end. The Stasi even tried to turn the couple's young son, Jonas, against them. It had instructed the headmistress of the school he attended to use her influence to get Jonas to spy on his parents.

The Stasi also used people's doctors against them. In 1983, Heinz Eggert, a Lutheran minister from Saxony, came down with dysentery while on vacation. Back home, he checked into a hospital, where the attending physician gave him a prescription that he said Eggert would have to take for the rest of his life. Even with the medication, however, Eggert's condition continued to worsen. He grew weaker and more depressed all the time. He gave up most of his human rights activities and even considered suicide. Then Eggert stopped taking the prescribed medication. His mental and physical condition began to improve again steadily! Eggert had not known what to make of the experience. His Stasi file now proved that the doctor in Saxony who had treated him had been ordered by the Stasi to prescribe a combination of amphetamines and tranquilizers that would weaken and depress him. One could only guess how many other cases of medical malpractice the Stasi had ordered—with perhaps deadly results.

Sometimes the information contained in the files bordered on the absurd. Lutz Rathenow was a poet who had fallen out of favor with the Communist government. Among the thousands pages of reports on his activities, there was one that read:

> Rathenow then crossed the street and ordered a sausage at the sausage stand. The following conversation took place. Rathenow: "A sausage please."
> Sausage Seller: " With or without rolls?"
> Rathenow: "With, please." Sausage Seller: "And mustard?" Rathenow: "Yes, with mustard."
> Further exchange of words did not take place.[1]

The Stasi seemed to have an insatiable appetite for the most insignificant details of the lives of more than 6 million East Germans: what they ate for breakfast, how often they took out the trash, the names of their dogs and cats, even where they stored their ironing boards. Yet, in spite of the vast archives they had accumulated, the leaders of the GDR were unable to anticipate the great changes that swept the country and brought the Communist government crashing to the ground in 1989.

▼ ▲ ▼

In addition to making a decision about Stasi files, the German government faced the question of how to deal with the former leaders of the GDR, especially Erich Honecker. Shortly after his removal from power in November 1989, Honecker was placed under house arrest at his spacious home at Wandlitz. Within a few weeks, however, Communist leaders were forced to move out of their compound at Wandlitz. Honecker sought refuge at the home of a Lutheran minister in the city of Lobetal, to the north of the capital. Shortly after that, Honecker was moved to the Soviet military hospital at Berlitz. Reports that he was very ill with cancer began to filter out.

On the night of March 14, 1991, Honecker was carried onto a Soviet jet and secretly flown to Moscow. Soviet officials said that they had taken the action for "humanitarian reasons" and that the condition of the 78-year-old Honecker had taken a sudden turn for the worse. German officials, however, denounced the Soviet action as gross interference in Germany's internal affairs and demanded Honecker's return. A diplomatic standoff continued for several months. Frederich Wolff, Honecker's lawyer, predicted that the former German leader would probably spend the remainder of his days in the Soviet Union.

By the end of 1991, however, the Soviet Union had ceased to exist, and those who had approved Honecker's removal to the Soviet Union, including Mikhail Gorbachev, were no longer in power. The new Russian government of President Boris Yeltsin made it very clear that they considered Honecker subject to arrest and deportation to Germany.

To escape trial in Germany, Erich Honecker secretly flew to Moscow.

Confused and ill, Honecker made his way with his wife to the Chilean embassy in Moscow. His daughter had married a man from Chile and now made her home in South America. Honecker asked the Chilean government for permission to live with his daughter. Chile refused to grant Honecker's request. However, the Chilean ambassador, Clodomiro Almeyda, had been granted refuge in East Berlin when the military dictator Augusto Pinochet had taken over Chile in 1973. Almeyda felt he owed Honecker a favor, and so he allowed the ailing Communist to remain in the embassy temporarily. Because international law forbids the police of a nation from entering foreign embassies on their soil without permission, Honecker would be safe from arrest by Russian police—and from deportation to Germany—as long as he remained inside the embassy.

Honecker remained at the Chilean embassy for seven months. Finally, in July 1992, under pressure from both Germany and Russia, Almeyda had to inform his guest that his grace period was over and that he would have to leave. On July 29, Russian police handed Honecker over to German authorities, who flew him back to Berlin. The former leader was then driven by limousine to the capital's Central Detention Center, where he was fingerprinted, photographed, and told to change into the official prison uniform. He was to share a cell with a gypsy accused of armed robbery.

Honecker's trial began in Berlin on November 12. His codefendants included Erich Mielke, the former head of the Stasi; Heinz Kessler, a former defense minister; and Willi Stoph, a former prime minister of the GDR. Honecker was officially charged with corruption and manslaughter in connection with the deaths of 49 East Germans who had been killed while trying to flee the Communist regime. According to the German prosecutors, Honecker was liable in these deaths because he had issued the orders to the GDR's border guards that they should shoot to kill those who tried to leave; he had also ordered that explosive devices be buried in the "death strip" along the eastern side of the Berlin Wall.

The trial was delayed for several days when Stoph suffered a heart attack. The presiding judge ruled that the former prime minister would be tried separately at a later date. When the trial resumed on November 17, Honecker fainted as he was being led into the courtroom. A doctor examined him and noted that the former leader's blood pressure was abnormally high and that his heart was beating irregularly. Once again, the trial was recessed, and Honecker was taken to a prison hospital. The German magazine *Der Spiegel* began to refer to the trial of Honecker and the other elderly Communist leaders as "a race against death."[2]

For some time, Honecker's lawyers had been trying to have the case of the former leader dismissed because of Honecker's poor health. According to several doctors who had examined him, Honecker was terminally ill with stomach cancer and probably had only a few months to live. On January 13, 1993, Germany's supreme court agreed. It ruled that Honecker was too ill to stand trial and that keeping him in prison any longer would be a violation of his human rights. Charges against Honecker were dismissed, and he was allowed to join his family in Chile.

Reaction to this turn of events was mixed. Many Germans were relieved that the country would be spared the spectacle of seeing the old, frail Honecker on trial. Others, however, felt they had been duped—especially when they saw news footage of Honecker's arrival in Santiago de Chile. Not only had the old leader survived the 20-hour flight across the Atlantic, but he walked down the airplane steps under his own power, his hat in his hands, at what many felt was an amazingly brisk pace for a man with only "a few months" to live. At the bottom of the stairs, he was greeted warmly by family members and friends, then stopped for a few minutes to give an interview to a reporter from a Chilean newspaper. Yes, Honecker told the reporter, he had "high hopes" for his future—and for the future of socialism. While he was in Chile, he added, he would continue work on his memoirs. Soon, however, Honecker's health began to decline again. He died in Santiago on May 29, 1994.

▼ ▲ ▼

Just as figures from the immediate past caused troubles, so older disturbing memories surfaced for Germany—ghosts from the years before the Communist takeover in the East, from Germany's Nazi past.

Beginning in 1990, the number of violent crimes against foreigners in Germany had begun to rise steadily. For years, West Germany had been a haven for immigrants from other countries. When the Communist system throughout Eastern Europe fell in late 1989, immigrants from those lands sought new homes in Germany.

By the summer of 1992, well over 1,000 refugees a day were streaming into Germany—a rate of almost a half a million a year. German immigration law was the most generous in Europe, promising all of the new arrivals housing, clothing, medical care, and food while their applications were being processed. In addition to those who wanted to live there permanently, Germany continued to welcome thousands of guest workers from southern and eastern Europe. In past years, these temporary workers had helped to make up for West Germany's severe labor shortage. Now their presence was deeply resented by many East Germans, millions of whom were now without jobs due to the business closings caused by unification.

In August of 1992, there were outbursts of violence against foreigners in numerous German cities. On the night of August 24, a group of several hundred young people armed with clubs and iron bars attacked a hostel for foreign workers in the northeastern port city of Rostock. The police quickly moved to evacuate 200 Romanian gypsies who were being housed temporarily at the hostel—and not a moment too soon. A short while later, the mob broke into the building and burned it to the ground. All the while a large crowd of Rostock citizens cheered enthusiastically. When police moved in later to retake control of the area, fierce fighting between the youths and police broke out. It continued for nearly a week.

By Wednesday night the violence had spread to other eastern German cities. In Eberswalde, an industrial suburb northeast of Berlin, about 150 members of a group called Comrades for Comradeship Eberswalde marched to the foreigners' hostel in that city, chanting "Sieg Heil" and raising their arms in the Nazi salute. Similar harassment of foreigners was also reported at Frankfurt an der Oder, a city on the border with Poland.

Violence marked the next two weekends as well. On the evenings of September 4, 5, and 6, large crowds of antiforeigner demonstrators protested outside hostels in communities all along Germany's eastern border: at Cottbus, Kolkwitz, Spremberg, Lübbenau, and Hoterswerda. Similar reports were received from

In a demonstration against antiforeigner violence, protesters carry a sign reading, "Stop the reestablishment of the 4th Reich."

several cities near Berlin, and renewed fighting in the streets of Rostock was also reported.

Shocked by the violent protests, Manfred Stolpe, now the premier of the eastern *Land* of Brandenburg, traveled to Cottbus and called a public meeting of concerned citizens. He was there to listen rather than to speak, Stolpe told the crowd, but he warned them: "This is how something began that ended at Auschwitz." Stolpe was referring to the Nazi extermination camp, just 200 miles away in Poland. "These riots are the worst thing that have happened in Germany since 1945," Stolpe continued, "a scandal for our whole country. We are not neo-Nazis. We want to live together with others."[3]

But, in spite of Stolpe's words, the crowd continued to pour out its anger against foreigners. The politicians did not understand what it was like for people to be afraid to walk down the street because of rising crime, one man said. "They live in villas in Bonn and Berlin, where nobody uses their lawn for a toilet." The crowd was also addressed by a Frank Hübner, who had founded a right-wing organization called German Alternative. While Hübner admitted that he was a "national socialist," he denied that his organization was behind the recent violence. "But we are going to stand up and support the right of citizens who want to walk the streets safely," Hübner declared.[4]

Many Germans agreed with Stolpe, however, and feared that hate crimes against foreigners could lead to a resurgence of Nazi ideas within Germany. But even among those opposed to right-wing violence, there were wide differences.

On November 8, 1992, more than 300,000 Germans came to Berlin for a mass rally called by the government to oppose violence against foreigners. However, what was meant to be a great show of German unity became instead yet another illustration of German discord. Radical elements within the crowd pelted President Richard von Welzsäcker with eggs, tomatoes, sticks, rocks, and paint bombs as he stood on the platform. His attempts to address the crowd were drowned out by cries of "Hypocrites! Liars!" and by shrill whistles, which prevented the press microphones from picking up Welzsäcker's speech. A short while later, Chancellor Helmut Kohl was pelted with eggs as he walked with the crowd down Berlin's main avenue, Unter den Linden, and through the Brandenburg Gate.

As the events of the day were concluding, Ignatz Bubis, head of the Central Council of Jews in Germany, mounted the platform to express the anger many felt. "I am ashamed of what has happened here," Bubis said sternly. "We are not in 1938—we are in 1992. Violence can only take us to the abyss."[5]

Most Germans agreed with the sentiments expressed by Bubis, and the government moved quickly to outlaw several leading neo-Nazi organizations, including the Nationalist Movement and Frank Hübner's German Alternative. But right-wing violence continued to rise. Many young people in particular, without the memories of the terror the Nazis had once unleashed on Germany and the world, seemed drawn to totalitarianism's easy answers and handy scapegoats. Among the hit songs of the musical group Störkraft ("Destructive Force") was one song called "Kraft für Deutschland" ("Strength for Germany"):

> *We fight shaved, our fists are hard as steel,*
> *Our hearts beat true for our Fatherland.*
> *Whatever may happen, we will never leave you.*
> *We will stand true for our Germany,*
> *Because we are the strength for Germany*
> *That makes Germany clean...*

The song concluded: "Deutchland wachen" ("Germany awake!").[6] "Germany awake!" was the same slogan the Nazis had chanted in the years just before they seized power.

chapter 10

Heading For the Future

During the 40 years of Communist rule, schoolchildren in East Germany had never been taught the words of their country's national anthem. Instead, they had been instructed merely to hum the tune as the nation's flag was raised. But now, with their country united again, they could sing out at full voice:

> *Arisen out of the ruins and headed for the future,*
> *Let us serve Germany, our united fatherland.*

The euphoria that followed the fall of the Berlin Wall and the rapid reunification of Germany soon gave way to a more realistic attitude. With the exception of the Soviet Union, united Germany was the most populous nation in Europe. In geographic area, only the USSR, France, and Spain were larger. Many predicted that Germany would emerge as the continent's economic powerhouse, with the highest value of exported goods of any nation in the entire world.

But the idea of a united, strong Germany, dominating the heart of Europe, caused many to worry. Twice before in the twentieth century, uncontrolled German nationalism had led to war. In the years since the end of World War II, the Federal Republic had emerged as a peaceful, stable member of the Western alliance. In spite of occasional rivalries over economic policies and trade, West Germany maintained good relations with all of its neighbors and an especially close relationship with the United States. Now, some feared that an expanded Federal Republic might develop into a Fourth Reich—a fourth German Empire—setting the historical stage for future tragedy.

But many others believed that such fears were misplaced. They pointed out that there were vast differences between the Federal Republic and the Weimar government whose collapse had given rise to Hitler. Weimar had been an economic weakling, never able to emerge from the devastation and indebtedness of the First World War. The Federal Republic ranked among the economically strongest nations in the world. The Weimar government had faced the enormous burden of having to pay billions of dollars in reparations to victorious Entente. The FRG *received* billions of dollars in assistance from the Western Allies, whose chief goal was to rebuild West Germany as quickly as possible. Democracy had never taken firm root in Germany under the Weimar constitution. Its leaders had been looked upon by many of their fellow Germans as traitors who had surrendered the country to its enemies. The FRG, on the other hand, had grown into a lively democratic state, where elections were hotly contested, civil rights were strictly protected, and strong democratic institutions were steadfastly maintained.

During peacetime, the FRG had flourished. Its people enjoyed one of the highest standards of living in the world. And it was to gain access to this economic prosperity—and not out of any hunger for political domination or national glorification—that the people of the East supported the cause of reunification so resolutely. One observer made just this point in this description of the night the Wall fell:

> *Amid popping champagne corks, the emotions were*
> *those of a family reunion—not the bloody-minded*
> *reflexes of unshackled nationalism. People got*
> *drunk on booze, not* Volk *and* Vaterland. . . . *In*
> *West Germany, nobody was thronging through the*
> *streets of Frankfurt, Munich, or Hamburg to clam-*

our for Anschluss. *Indeed,* nobody *was march-
ing—except those East Germans who streamed
through the Wall with the incredulous wonderment
that might befall inmates suddenly left in charge of
a jailhouse. No* Deutschland *raised their heart-
beats, but kiwis and bananas, those symbols of
untasted luxury which they carted home by the
bushel. . . . And in the minds of East Germans
[Kohl's] message read not* Deutschland über alles
but Deutschmark über alles.[1]

"We have learned our historical lesson," Germans told those
who expressed nervousness about expanded German nationalism. The spectre of 70 million people killed in two world wars
would be enough to check the rise of Fourth Reich.

▼ ▲ ▼

There were, however, a few unsettling signs. In spite of the
German government's efforts and a stricter immigration law,
which slowed the tide of refugees seeking to live in the
Federal Republic, violence against foreigners continued to
rise. In April 1994, four young neo-Nazis were found guilty
of firebombing a hostel for foreigners in the western town of
Solingen, near the industrial city of Düsseldorf. The bombing killed five Turkish women and girls, all members of the
same family.

On the rise too were antisemitism and acts of violence against
Jews—crimes that memories of the Holocaust had largely kept in
check for more than 40 years. Although the Jewish population of
Germany in 1990 numbered only around 30,000, compared to
over 600,000 prior to World War II, the West German government
had worked hard with leaders of the German Jewish community to
keep alive the memory of past tragedies and to prevent similar
occurrences in the future.

However, as the condition of the German economy worsened in the months that followed unity, some Germans again looked to "the Jews" for a scapegoat for their nation's woes. Early in 1991 the grave of the German writer Bertolt Brecht was smeared with the words "*Sau Jude raus!*" ("Pig Jew, get out!"), though Brecht was not Jewish. A few months later a monument to the 55,000 Berlin Jews killed by the Nazis was overturned. Swastikas and anti-Jewish slogans were painted on several Jewish synagogues. In March 1994, the synagogue in the northern port city of Lübeck was firebombed—just a few days before its members were to hold their first Passover seder since the Holocaust. Even more ominous than these somewhat scattered reports of violence and vandalism were the results of a public opinion poll conducted in Germany on behalf of the American Jewish Committee. Of the 1,400 German adults questioned, more than 20 percent said they had negative feelings about Jews. More than one third maintained that the Holocaust was an event of the past, irrelevant to modern life. And nearly 50 percent believed that antisemitism in Germany would continue to rise with the passage of time.

The German government moved quickly to meet the challenge. The nation's highest judicial body, the Constitutional Court, held that freedom of speech in Germany did not extend to those who claimed that the Holocaust had never occurred. The court deemed the so-called Auschwitz Lie—the neo-Nazi claim that the Holocaust is a myth created by Jews and other foreigners to discredit Germany—a "proven untruth," and so not covered by the German constitution's guarantee of freedom of speech for all citizens.

Still, a relatively small number of extreme rightists in Germany seemed intent in stirring up past hatreds. Sometimes they helped to create tensions both within the boundaries of the FRG and beyond them. In April 1994 a British sports association canceled a soccer match between British and German teams because it was to be held in Berlin on April 20—the anniversary of Hitler's birth. Right-wing extremists in the German capital had held large rallies on that date in past years. The match was also to be held in Berlin's Olympic Stadium, which had been especially built by Hitler in 1936 as a showcase of Nazism. In canceling the event, British sports officials cited their fear that the match would be disrupted by modern-day admirers of Hitler.

As the fiftieth anniversary of World War II approached, the Allied governments made plans for events to commemorate their victories. In June of 1994 the Allies were to gather in Normandy on the coast of France, to mark the fiftieth anniversary of D Day, the day of the Allied landings in France that many cite as an important turning point in the war. According to some sources, Chancellor Helmut Kohl wanted very much to be invited to the festivities. Such an invitation, he thought, would serve as the "great pardon" for which Germans had yearned since the war ended. It would be a clear indication that the strife and conflict of the past were truly over and that Germany was fully welcome in the councils of Europe once again.

But Kohl received no such invitation. For many French veterans, especially, the sad era of German occupation could never be forgotten. The presence of the German chancellor at events commemorating that time would be just too bitter to swallow. There would be no "great pardon" for Kohl.

▼ ▲ ▼

The chancellor's political position seemed to weaken steadily as the happy days of revolution and reunification fell farther into the past. The man who had once been greeted as "the liberator of Leipzig" and "the father of German unity" now was derided with heckling and catcalls when he appeared before crowds in cities in the eastern part of the country. The recession that had gripped the country in 1992 showed few signs of lessening, and many blamed the policies of the Kohl government for the country's poor economic showing. New elections to the Bundestag were scheduled for October 1994. Most believed the chancellor's Christian

Democrats faced a difficult struggle in their quest for reelection. When the German people voted, however, they gave the chancellor a narrow electoral victory. Kohl's Christian Democratic Party and its smaller coalition partners, the Christian Social Union and the Free Democratic Party, would hold 341 seats in the new Bundestag. Opposition parties, including the Social Democrats, would hold just seven fewer, or 334, seats.

Just a month after the elections, on November 9, 1994, Germany observed the fifth anniversary of the fall of the Berlin Wall. Once again, there were celebrations in the streets of Berlin—though nowhere nearly as large as those of 1989. Once again, songs were sung. There was dancing, though not on top of the Wall this time, for the Wall was gone.

So was the Stasi. And Erich Honecker. And the Socialist Unity Party. And East German Communism. And East Germany itself, for that matter. All gone.

And gone too were all illusions that unity could come easily or cheaply. Or that the past could be readily forgotten. Or that the nightmare of Auschwitz could simply be banished from the German memory.

But Germany remained, united again: a powerful nation and a strong people, a major force in Europe—and the world.

Chapter Notes

Chapter 1
1. Angela Stent, "The One Germany," in *The Reunification of Germany*, ed. by Robert Emmet Long (New York: H. W. Wilson, 1992), 114.
2. *New York Times*, October 3, 1990, 17.
3. Ibid., 17.

Chapter 2
1. Otto Friedrich, "Germany: Toward Unity," *Time*, July 9, 1990, 69.
2. William L. Shirer, *The Rise and Fall of the Third Reich: A History of Nazi Germany* (New York: Simon and Schuster, 1960), 1104.

Chapter 3
1. Winston Churchill, "Winston Churchill Warns the West of the Soviet Iron Curtain," in *Lend Me Your Ears: Great Speeches in History*, ed. by William Safire (New York: W. W. Norton, 1992), 791.
2. Louis J. Halle, *The Cold War as History* (New York: Harper and Row, 1967), 365.
3. Ibid., 371.
4. Ibid., 396.

Chapter 4
1. Halle, *The Cold War as History*, 397.
2. Doris M. Epler, *The Berlin Wall: How It Rose and Why It Fell* (Brookfield, Connecticut: Millbrook Press, 1992), 60.
3. John F. Kennedy, "President John F. Kennedy Assures West Germany of America's Steadfastness," in *Lend Me Your Ears*, 494.
4. Ibid., 495.
5. Elizabeth Pond, *Beyond the Wall: Germany's Road to Unification* (Washington, D.C.: Brookings Institution, 1993), 82.

Chapter 5

1. Timothy Garton Ash, *The Magic Lantern: The Revolution of '89 Witnessed in Warsaw, Budapest, Berlin, and Prague* (New York: Random House, 1990), 65.
2. Mark Frankland, *The Patriots' Revolution: How Eastern Europe Toppled Communism and Won Its Freedom* (Chicago: Ivan R. Dee, 1992), 226.
3. *New York Times*, October 19, 1989, 1.
4. Epler, *The Berlin Wall*, 98.

Chapter 6

1. *New York Times*, November 11, 1989, 1.
2. Garton Ash, *The Magic Lantern*, 75.
3. *New York Times*, December 18, 1989, 14.
4. Ibid., 14.
5. Ibid., 14.
6. Robert Darnton, *Berlin Journal: 1989–1990* (New York: W. W. Norton, 1991), 261.
7. *New York Times*, April 13, 1990, 1.

Chapter 7

1. Pond, *Beyond the Wall*, 172.
2. Ibid., 222.
3. *New York Times*, September 13, 1990, 1.

Chapter 8

1. *New York Times*, March 12, 1991, 1.
2. *Bangor Daily News*, November 23, 1990, 6.
3. Ibid., 6.

Chapter 9

1. Stephen Kinzer, "East Germans Face Their Accusers," *New York Times Magazine*, April 12, 1992, 27.
2. *New York Times*, November 18, 1992, 8.
3. *New York Times*, September 6, 1992, 16.
4. Ibid., 16.
5. *New York Times*, December 2, 1992, 1.

Chapter 10

1. Josef Joffe, "One-and-a-Half Cheers for German Reunification," in *The Reunification of Germany*, 82.

Glossary

Allies—France, Great Britain, the Soviet Union, the United States, and the nations that sided with them against the Axis forces (Germany, Italy, Japan, and their supporters) during World War II.

capitalism—An economic system in which property is owned by private individuals or groups and the free market forces of supply and demand operate.

coalition—A group composed of members of two or more political parties who have joined forces to achieve common objectives.

Communism—An economic and political system in which all property is owned by the state and the society is placed under the control of a single (Communist) party.

conservative—An individual who is slow to embrace political and social change.

fascist—Referring to a political system characterized by a strong, authoritarian central government. The rights of opposition parties and individuals are severely limited.

liberalism—Belief in the desirability of change or reform in a system or institution.

Nazism—The political system founded in 1919, that under Adolf Hitler ruled Germany from 1933 to 1945. Its policies included a buildup in the German military; the annihilation of Jews, gypsies, and other groups; and the establishment of German supremacy over all Europe.

neo-Nazis—Proponents of beliefs and policies similar to those of the Nazis, including the supremacy of the white race, anti-semitism, and opposition to foreigners.

socialism—An economic and social system in which all property is owned in common for the good of the whole society.

Stalinism—A strict form of Communism, under which the rule of the Communist party leadership is tightly maintained and opposing viewpoints are severely repressed.

Time Line

1000 B.C.   Tribes from northern Europe begin to settle in the area that is now Germany.

A.D. 9   Germanic tribes defeat the Roman army at the Teutoburg Forest. Emperor Caesar Augustus gives up his plan to bring *Germani* under Roman control.

476   The German leader Odoacer defeats the last emperor of the Western Roman Empire, Romulus Augustulus. The lands of the Western Roman Empire are divided among various tribes.

800   The Frankish king Charlemagne is crowned emperor of a new Western Empire, with its capital in the German city Aachen. In 806, Charlemagne divides his empire among his three sons. When his last surviving son, Louis dies in 814, the empire is divided yet again, among Louis's three sons.

1138   Conrad III of Swabia establishes the Hohenstaufen dynasty, which becomes one of the most powerful forces in Europe. With its collapse in 1263, however, Germany again divides into scores of separate political entities.

1517   Martin Luther, a German monk, criticizes the Catholic Church. When many German princes side with him, the Protestant Reformation is launched.

1555   The Peace of Augsburg gives each German prince the right to determine the religion in his own territory.

1618   The Thirty Years' War between Europe's Catholics
        and Protestants begins.

1740   Frederick the Great becomes king of Prussia. He
        rules until 1786 and greatly extends the territory and
        influence of the Hohenzollern dynasty.

1806   The French emperor Napoleon abolishes the Holy
        Roman Empire and establishes the Confederation of
        the Rhine, a union of 16 different German states, in
        its place. Frederick Wilhelm III of Prussia declares
        war on France, but his armies are defeated at the
        battle of Jena. As a result, Prussia loses much of its
        territory.

1813   Napoleon is defeated at the Battle of the Nations,
        near Leipzig, by an alliance of Great Britain,
        Prussia, Russia, Sweden, and Spain.

1815   Napoleon's attempt to regain power is halted at
        Waterloo. The Congress of Vienna establishes a new
        German Confederation.

1862   King Wilhelm of Prussia names Otto von Bismark
        prime minister.

1867   A new North German Confederation, dominated by
        Prussia, is formed.

1871   Prussia defeats France in the six-week Franco-
        Prussian war, and King Wilhelm is proclaimed
        kaiser of a new German Empire. Bismark is named
        chancellor.

1914   World War I begins.

1918   With his people in rebellion and his armed forces in mutiny, Kaiser Wilhelm II abdicates and flees the country on November 9. A new German Republic is established. On November 11, the German military command surrenders, bringing World War I to a close.

1919   A new German constitution is adopted at Weimar. The Treaty of Versailles imposes harsh terms of peace on Germany.

1921   Runaway inflation wreaks havoc on the German economy.

1929   Germany's economy is further weakened as a result of the Great Depression.

1934   Hindenburg dies; Hitler names himself Führer and declares the establishment of the Third Reich.

1933   In January, President Hindenburg names the Nazi leader Adolf Hitler chancellor. Following the Reichstag fire the next month, the Enabling Acts are passed, laying the foundation for the Nazi dictatorship.

1936   Germany invades the Rhineland, in violation of the Versailles Treaty.

1938   Germany annexes Austria and, under the Munich Agreement, gains control of the Sudetenland from Czechoslovakia.

1939   In March the world does nothing as Hitler seizes the rest of Czechoslovakia. However, when Germany invades Poland in September, World War II begins.

1940   Germany occupies Denmark, Norway, Belgium, the
             Netherlands, and France.

1941   Germany occupies Yugoslavia and Greece, and Hitler
             launches the invasion of the Soviet Union.

1944   The Allied landing in Normandy (D Day) opens the
             second front in Europe.

1945   In the face of his armies' certain defeat, Hitler kills
             himself. Germany surrenders. The Potsdam
             Declaration lays down principles for the Allied occu-
             pation of Germany.

1948   France, Great Britain, and the United States launch
             the Berlin airlift in response to the Soviet blockade of
             West Berlin.

1949   Federal Republic of Germany (West Germany) is
             established, with its capital at Bonn; Konrad
             Adenauer is elected chancellor. The Soviet Zone in
             the east becomes the German Democratic Republic,
             under the leadership of Communist party leader
             Walter Ulbricht.

1953   A workers' uprising in East Germany is put down by
             Soviet troops.

1961   In response to a rapid rise in the number of refugees
             fleeing to the West, the Communist government of
             East Germany erects the Berlin Wall.

1963   President John F. Kennedy speaks at the Berlin Wall
             and assures the people of West Berlin of the West's
             support.

1969   Willi Brandt, mayor of West Berlin, becomes West
              German chancellor and launches his policies of
              Ostpolitik, or closer relations with the East.

1971   Erich Honecker replaces Walter Ulbricht as leader of
              East Germany. The United States, the Soviet Union,
              Great Britain, and France sign the Four Powers
              Agreement, which guarantees the existence of two
              separate, sovereign German states, and guarantees
              access to West Berlin.

1985   Mikhail Gorbachev comes to power in the Soviet
              Union and launches his programs of *glasnost* and
              perestroika.

1988   The East German government intensifies its repres-
              sion as the country's human rights movement gains
              momentum. The sale of Soviet publications in the
              GDR is banned.

1989   (Summer) East German refugees pack the West
              German embassies in Budapest, Prague, and Warsaw,
              seeking to migrate to the West.

              (September) Exodus of refugees increases when
              Hungary officially opens its borders with Austria.
              Reform group New Forum is founded in Leipzig.

              (October) Following the celebrations marking the for-
              tieth anniversary of the founding of the GDR, demon-
              strations against Honecker's government break out in
              cities across the country. On October 18, Honecker is
              replaced as Communist leader by Egon Krenz.

              (November) Demonstrations against the government
              continue to spread. On November 9 the East German

government announces a lifting of restrictions on travel to the West, making the Berlin Wall obsolete.

(December) The leading role of the Communist party is removed from the GDR's constitution. Krenz resigns and is replaced by Gregor Gysi, who presents the party's new "Revolutionary Program." New political parties are formed in East Germany.

1990   (March) Alliance for Germany wins the first free East German elections on a platform of rapid reunification with the West.

(April) Lothar de Maizière forms the first non-Communist government in the GDR's history.

(May) Two Plus Four talks, aimed at German reunification, begin.

(July) East and West German economies are merged. Gorbachev lifts his objection to German membership in NATO.

(September) Two Plus Four talks are completed with the signing in Moscow of a final treaty on reunification.

(October) German reunification becomes official.

Selected
Bibliography

Beschloss, Michael R. *The Crisis Years: Kennedy and Khrushchev, 1960-1963*. New York: HarperCollins, Edward Burlingame Books, 1991.

Bond, Martyn. *A Tale of Two Germanys*. Wilmington, Delaware: Atomium Books, 1990.

Bornstein, Jerry. *The Wall Came Tumbling Down: The Berlin Wall and the Fall of Communism*. New York: Arch Cape Press, 1990.

Broszat, Martin. *Hitler and the Collapse of Weimar Germany*. Leamington Spa, England: Berg Books, 1987.

Darnton, Robert. *Berlin Journal: 1989–1990*. New York: W. W. Norton, 1991.

Epler, Doris M. *The Berlin Wall: How It Rose and Why It Fell*. Brookfield, Connecticut: Millbrook Press, 1992.

Frankland, Mark. *The Patriots' Revolution: How Eastern Europe Toppled Communism and Won Its Freedom*. Chicago: Ivan R. Dee, 1992.

Fulbrook, Mary. *A Concise History of Germany*. Cambridge, England: Cambridge University Press: 1990.

Garton Ash, Timothy. *In Europe's Name: Germany and the Divided Continent*. New York: Random House, 1993.

Garton Ash, Timothy. *The Magic Lantern: The Revolution of '89 Witnessed in Warsaw, Budapest, Berlin, and Prague.* New York: Random House, 1990.

Gelb, Norman. *The Berlin Wall: Kennedy, Khrushchev, and a Showdown in the Heart of Europe.* New York: Times Books, 1986.

Gwertzman, Bernard and Michael T. Kaufman, eds. *The Collapse of Communism.* New York: Times Books, 1990.

Halle, Louis J. *The Cold War as History.* New York: Harper and Row, 1967.

Jarausch, Konrad H. *The Rush to German Unity.* New York: Oxford University Press, 1994.

Kahler, Erich. *The Germans.* Princeton: Princeton University Press, 1974.

Long, Robert Emmet, ed. *The Reunification of Germany.* New York: H. W. Wilson, 1992.

McAdams, A. James. *Germany Divided: From the Wall to Reunification.* Princeton: Princeton University Press, 1993.

Pond, Elizabeth. *Beyond the Wall: Germany's Road to Unification.* Washington D.C.: Brookings Institution, 1993.

Shirer, William L. *The Rise and Fall of the Third Reich: A History of Nazi Germany.* New York: Simon and Schuster, 1960.

Stokes, Gale. *The Walls Came Tumbling Down.* New York: Oxford University Press, 1993.

Turner, Henry Ashby. *The Two Germanies Since 1945.* New Haven: Yale University Press, 1987.

Index

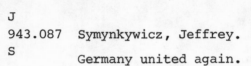